# THE DEEP WORK SOCIETY

## Book One

# The Book On
# The Myth of Multitasking

## The Book On Series

## By Anonymous

Published by The Book On Publishing, 2025.

First edition. June 20, 2025.

Website: https://thebookon.ca

Substack: https://thebookonpublishing.substack.com/

While every precaution has been taken in the preparation of this book, the publisher assumes no responsibility for errors or omissions, or damages resulting from the use of the information contained herein.

THE MYTH OF MULTITASKING

First edition. June 20, 2025.



Written by Anonymous.

# The Book On Series

The Book On Life Unscripted
The Book On Risk Management in Payments
The Book On AI for Everyday People
The Book On Relationships
The Book On Master The Algorithm
The Book On Saying No
The Book On Community Led Strategy
The Book On The Myth of Multitasking
The Book On The Burnout Blueprint
The Book On The Digital Reboot
The Book On The Shape of What's Coming
The Book On Strategic Obsession
The Book On High-Stakes Thinking
The Book On Artificial Leverage
The Book On Clarity
The Book On Uncertainty
The Book On Operational Excellence
The Book On Escape

# Table of Contents

# Read This First

This is not a book designed to entertain you. It's not here to charm, to soothe, or to hold your hand. It won't dazzle you with stories, metaphors, or motivational fluff. What you're having is a tool, an instruction manual written for people who are serious about learning, executing, and thinking at a higher level.

Every book in The Book On Series is built on a single premise: clarity beats complexity. We believe that when you strip away the noise, the emotions, the marketing spin, and the cultural rituals of "self-help," what's left is raw, unembellished instruction. That's what these books offer.

They are dry by design. Not because we don't care about language or narrative, but because when you're building something that matters, you don't need more distractions. You need a clear architecture. Mental scaffolding. Direction that respects your intelligence.

Each title in this series takes on a specific domain: decision-making, clarity, strategy, leverage, and uncertainty, and drills deep. Not in sweeping generalizations, but in applied frameworks. These are books for builders, operators, founders, tacticians, and thinkers—people who don't just consume knowledge but operationalize it.

You'll find no chapter-long anecdotes here. No self-congratulatory memoirs. No bullet-point platitudes. Instead, what you'll get is structured insight: argument, example, application.

The tone is direct. The prose is sober. The ideas are designed to be lifted out and used.

You won't be coddled, but you won't be misled either.

There's a place in the world for lyrical, emotional, story-driven books, and this isn't that place. This is a workspace. A blueprint. A conversation for people who are ready to act, not just absorb.

We respect your time and your intellect.

Welcome to The Book On Series.

# Dedication

For anyone who's ever stared at a screen, surrounded by noise, and quietly wondered, *"Why can't I think anymore?"*
This book is for you.
And the part of you still capable of deep focus, even if the world forgot to make space for it.
- Anonymous.

# Epigraph

"You can do anything, but not everything."
— David Allen

# Preface

You probably don't need another book telling you you're distracted.

You already know. You can feel it in the way your thoughts don't land like they used to. In how hard it's become to finish a page, a paragraph—even a sentence—without the itch to check something. You sense it when you talk to people you love and realize you were only half there, when your brain feels full and empty at the same time.

You're not broken. You're overloaded.

And the overload is no accident. We live in a world engineered for interruption. A culture that confuses motion with meaning, responsiveness with value, hustle with purpose. We've been told that doing more at once is a sign of strength. The idea is that saying yes to everything is how you get ahead. That presence is optional—but productivity is sacred.

It's a lie. And it's costing us more than we realize.

This book is not about time management. It's not about willpower or morning routines or finding the perfect productivity app. It's about reclaiming the one resource that determines the quality of everything you do: your attention.

*The Myth of Multitasking* is the first part of a trilogy called *The Deep Work Society*. It's about living deliberately in an age of digital frenzy. This first book will help you understand what multitasking is, how it quietly fractures your memory, mood, and creativity—and what it takes to build a life around presence instead.

What follows is not a list of hacks. It's a remembering. A way to return to the parts of yourself you may have forgotten in the blur of constant input and divided focus.

This isn't about doing less. It's about doing what matters, fully.

Let's begin.

# Part I: The Problem We Live Inside

## Chapter 1: The Lie We've Learned to Live

I wasn't planning to forget my wedding anniversary.

It wasn't because I didn't care. I did. Deeply. I had even written a note to myself on a sticky pad two nights before. I'd thought about what kind of wine to pick up. I'd remembered a conversation where my wife had said, "No gifts, just time. Real time." The irony is that I was in the middle of preparing a keynote about work-life balance. I had every app open—Slack buzzing. Emails pinging. Calendar full. I was everywhere, except where I needed to be.

That's when it hit me: I wasn't forgetful. I was fractured.

And so are you.

You don't need a neuroscientist to tell you what your body already knows. You're tired, not because you don't sleep. You're slow, not because you're lazy. You're overwhelmed, not because you're weak. The modern myth is pulling you apart, that the more you do at once, the more you're getting done.

Multitasking isn't just a productivity lie. It's a lifestyle lie. And we've built an entire society on top of it.

We reward it. We celebrate people who hustle, juggle, and run between meetings, all while answering texts and "listening" to their kids talk about their day. We fill out résumés with words like "multitasker" and treat it like a badge of honour. We pride ourselves on being reachable at any hour, across any device. We say yes to everything and then apologize to everyone because we've given them all a fraction of ourselves.

But here's the thing: multitasking isn't real. Not the way we think it is. What we call multitasking is *rapid task-switching*, and it comes with a cost. Every time your brain moves from email to conversation to spreadsheet to news alert, it's using precious cognitive fuel. You're not splitting your attention; you're draining it and scattering the debris.

This isn't just anecdotal. Study after study shows the human brain can't focus on multiple complex tasks at once. People who think they're good at multitasking tend to perform *worse* than those who admit they struggle. Researchers at Stanford University found that heavy multitaskers were less able to filter out irrelevant information, had worse memory retention, and were slower at task-switching. The more they did, the less effective they became.

Let that sink in.

We've convinced ourselves we're optimizing our lives when, in fact, we're vandalizing our ability to live them.

It's not your fault. The world is built to distract you. Apps are designed with the same neuroscience used to make slot machines addictive. Notifications are weaponized attention hooks— workplaces reward availability over depth. We carry our entire social and professional world in a device that fits in our pocket, and it beeps every 14 minutes, if not more.

So we bounce between tasks not because we're irresponsible, but because the modern environment is engineered to keep us divided. Division keeps us docile. Distraction keeps us consuming. Shallow work makes us predictable. Focus, on the other hand, is threatening. It leads to truth. It leads to clarity. It leads to change.

And that's what this book is about.

It's not a screed against technology. It's not a pitch for going off the grid or deleting your social media. It's a call to remember what it means to do one thing well. To work like an artisan. To think without interruption. To reclaim your ability to follow a thought from beginning to end without breaking it into pieces to keep up with a pace no one asked for, but everyone obeys.

You may feel broken. But you're not broken. You're overloaded. And the overload is coming from a world that treats your attention like a commodity instead of a gift.

In the pages ahead, we'll unpack how we got here, why multitasking became a myth we believed, and how to unlearn it. We'll explore the psychology of focus, the economics of attention, and the ancient truths buried beneath our obsession with productivity. Most importantly, we'll talk about what it means to build a life around depth, where your presence is no longer scattered, but grounded.

We can't slow the world down. But we can choose to move differently inside it.

And that begins by naming the myth.

This is how we start.

# Chapter 2: A Thousand Tabs Open

I once counted how many tabs I had open across all my devices in a single workday. Not metaphorically, literally. It was a quiet Tuesday morning when I decided to track it—thirty-seven browser tabs across two monitors. Six apps are running in the background. Slack, Zoom, and three separate email inboxes. Music streaming on my phone. Group texts pinging every few minutes. A running grocery list in Notes. A podcast paused mid-sentence because I'd "meant to get back to it later."

Thirty-seven digital tabs. And that didn't count the mental ones.

That day, I couldn't remember what I had eaten for lunch, just that I ate it standing, distracted, while reading a comment thread that made me feel anxious for no discernible reason. I ended the day drained, unsatisfied, and full of the gnawing sense that I had been busy without doing anything of substance. I had been everywhere but present. Engaged with everything and absorbed by nothing.

You know that feeling. It's the silent hum of modern life: too many inputs, too little meaning.

It's not just the browser tabs, apps, or pings. It's what they represent: an internalized mode of living that rewards splintering. We are no longer taught to follow one thread of thought from beginning to end. We are taught to live like devices, handling many windows at once, tolerating constant interruptions, optimizing everything for speed, and forgetting that deep work, deep thought, and deep living don't happen in slices. They occur in silence. In continuity.

Multitasking isn't just what we do. It's become who we are expected to be.

And that expectation starts young. Children today grow up swiping screens before they can write their names. They learn to toggle between assignments and social apps on the same device. Teens report anxiety when asked to complete tasks without background stimulation, music, TV, or simultaneous chatting. In school, attention is divided between tabs for homework and tabs for YouTube. And we reward this with praise: "You're such a great multitasker!" As if that were a compliment instead of a warning.

The most disturbing part? We've normalized this. Most people I speak to, intelligent, capable, driven people, don't even question the fractured nature of their days anymore. They see exhaustion as a personality trait, forgetfulness as a joke. "I can't even finish a book anymore," they'll say with a laugh. But beneath the humour, you can feel the ache—the loss. The quiet realization that something essential has gone missing, and no app is going to bring it back.

The deeper issue isn't that we're overloaded. It's that we've internalized overload as a form of value. We equate being in demand with being important. We think saying yes to everything will protect us from being left behind. We confuse responsiveness with responsibility. We chase every ping like a lifeline, afraid that missing one might cost us something, a deal, a friend, a piece of relevance.

But this chasing comes at a cost.

A 2022 study by the University of California, Irvine, found that once interrupted, it takes an average of **23 minutes and 15**

**seconds** to return to the original task fully. That's not because we're slow; it's because our attention has inertia. It requires momentum. When we stop and start, stop and start, over and over again, our brain doesn't just recover; it has to re-activate neural pathways from scratch.

And we do these dozens, sometimes hundreds of times per day.

We've traded focused effort for fractured output, and we wonder why we're exhausted before lunch.

And let's be honest: much of what we're switching between isn't meaningful. We're not toggling between life-saving decisions. We're flipping back and forth between responding to a non-urgent email, checking to see who viewed our story, googling something irrelevant, and wondering why we feel like we can't keep up. We aren't multitasking in the heroic sense of the word. We're scattering. Fraying. Losing small pieces of presence every time we shift focus for no real reason.

Imagine trying to write a book while someone taps your shoulder every 30 seconds. Or trying to have a meaningful conversation while a screen flashes random headlines in your peripheral vision. Or cooking a meal while a buzzer goes off every time someone likes your last photo. That's what our lives feel like now. And we've learned to call it "normal."

But it's not normal. It's unsustainable.

And the worst part? We've been sold this as *freedom*. Freedom to work anywhere. The freedom to choose our schedule. Freedom to be "on" at any hour. But what kind of freedom demands that you never entirely rest, never fully focus, never disconnect from the noise? That's not freedom. That's servitude dressed in sleek UX.

You don't need to quit your job or smash your phone to reclaim your brain. But you do need to stop pretending you're fine living with a thousand tabs open, both digitally and mentally. You are not a computer. You were never designed to run multiple programs simultaneously. And despite what the world tells you, your value doesn't come from how much you can handle at once. It comes from what you're able to bring your whole self to.

You know what that feels like. You've felt it in rare moments, when you were fully present in a conversation, lost in a book, immersed in a project, undistracted by noise. In those moments, there was clarity. Energy. Joy. That wasn't a fluke. That was your natural state, beneath the digital debris.

It's still in you.

The tabs will still be there tomorrow. But your mind? Your life? They're not infinite.

It's time to close a few.

# Chapter 3: The Cult of Busy

You ask someone how they're doing, and chances are, the first word out of their mouth will be "busy."

Not "happy." Not "fulfilled." Not "tired," though they almost certainly are. Just… "busy." It's become the default answer, not because it says much, but because it says *enough*. It says, *I matter*. It says, *I'm in motion*. It says, *Don't ask for more*. It's a shield disguised as a status symbol.

We have made the new badge of honour.

It didn't start this way. In generations past, status was tied to *leisure*. The wealthy were those who could afford not to be busy. Now, it's flipped. The more packed your calendar, the more meetings you juggle, the more plates you spin, the more valuable you're assumed to be. We no longer ask how well someone is doing; instead, we believe that if they're constantly busy, they must be important.

This is not harmless.

Busy has become a cultural addiction. We speak of it like the weather, inevitable, out of our control, mildly unpleasant but always present. "Things are crazy right now," we say, as though time and tasks happen to us like rainstorms. We romanticize exhaustion. We brag about how late we stayed up, how early we got up, how many tasks we crushed before breakfast. We treat burnout like a rite of passage, not a red flag.

But there's something deeper beneath the glorification of busy: fear.

Being busy is how we avoid ourselves. It's how we escape the uncomfortable quiet that asks, *What are you doing with your life?*

It's how we defer the big questions: Am I aligned with my values? Am I growing or just spinning my wheels? Am I living, or am I just filling my schedule with things that keep me from feeling stuck?

Busyness feels productive. But often, it's just well-camouflaged avoidance.

And here's the paradox: we often feel busiest when we're least effective. Why? Because busyness doesn't require intentionality. It just needs access. If your inbox is always open, your phone is always on, and your calendar is always editable, you will always be in motion but never in control. You'll move fast and go nowhere. You'll collapse at the end of the day, wondering what you accomplished.

This is the difference between motion and progress.

Motion is when you're doing a lot. Progress is when you're doing what matters.

Busy doesn't ask if something matters; it only asks *what's next*. It keeps your hands moving and your mind distracted, so you don't have to stop and ask the hard questions. But meaning never comes from motion alone. Meaning is quiet. It grows in stillness. It requires space, mental, emotional, and physical. Busyness crowds that space until there's no room left to think, reflect, or be.

One of the hardest things to do in a busy culture is to say, "I don't have anything on my schedule right now." People will look at you funny. Some will assume you're lazy, or drifting, or even depressed. The idea that someone might *protect* open time feels foreign to us. We've been conditioned to fill the silence, to schedule every hour, to believe that an empty calendar is a sign of a meaningless life.

But what if the opposite is true?

What if fullness isn't found in cramming more in, but in protecting what matters? What if the most critical work you do today is the quiet kind, thinking deeply, creating with intention, being fully present with someone you love? What if the highest form of success isn't being busy, but being *uninterrupted*?

We rarely stop to question the systems we serve. But busyness is a system. It feeds industries. The more rushed you feel, the more you crave shortcuts. The more overwhelmed you are, the more likely you are to outsource your thinking to an algorithm, a listicle, a promise of convenience. You become a consumer of solutions to a problem that the system created. And you pay for it, with your time, your attention, your peace of mind.

Escaping the cult of busy doesn't mean doing less for the sake of doing less. It means asking a better question: *Is what I'm doing aligned with who I want to become?*

Sometimes, deep work looks quiet. Sometimes, focus looks like space. And sometimes, the most courageous thing you can do in a frantic world is to slow down long enough to feel your heartbeat.

You are not a calendar. You are not a to-do list. You are not the number of unread emails you crushed today.

You are a human being. And you were never meant to live in a perpetual state of motion.

Busy is not a badge. It's a warning sign. And you don't have to wear it anymore.

# Chapter 4: We Called It Efficiency

We used to measure work by what we produced. Now, we measure it by how quickly we respond.

Somewhere along the line, speed became the standard. Fast replies. Fast pivots. Fast turnarounds. We started believing that if something wasn't moving, it was broken. Stillness began to feel like failure. Depth started to feel like inefficiency.

And so, in the name of efficiency, we made everything faster, but not necessarily better.

We called it progress when we could send emails from our wrists, hold meetings while commuting, and manage our entire lives from a screen the size of a deck of cards. We told ourselves we were optimizing. We created workflows, shortcuts, and stacks. We layered productivity on top of productivity, thinking that if we could find the right tool or the perfect routine, we'd finally get it all done.

But that's the trick of efficiency. It always promises peace but delivers pace.

The faster you move, the more you try to squeeze in. The more you squeeze in, the more fragmented your attention becomes. You may touch more things, but you hold nothing long enough to change it. Efficiency promises control but often steals clarity. We start confusing velocity with direction and end up racing toward nowhere in particular.

What we call efficiency is often just fragmentation in disguise.

This became obvious to me one morning during a "productivity sprint." I had blocked off two hours, turned off notifications, and lined up five tasks I was going to knock out back-to-back. No breaks, just output. On paper, I finished all five. But in the end, I didn't feel accomplished. I felt scrambled. I couldn't remember half of what I'd written. I didn't enjoy any of it. And what I had created, while technically done, lacked soul. I had moved through the list like a machine, fast, efficient, detached.

That's when it hit me: I wasn't doing real work. I was doing *task theatre*.

Task theatre is when you appear productive on the surface, with emails sent, meetings attended, and documents updated, but underneath, you're not making anything meaningful. You're performing the motions of a worker without engaging your mind in the work. You're crossing things off a list instead of contributing something new.

And because it *feels* like work, you keep doing it. You keep optimizing the show.

You automate your calendar. You shave seconds off your routine. You jump between tabs faster, speak in bullet points, and respond before thinking. You become efficient. But not effective.

You stop creating and start coordinating.

You stop thinking and start reacting.

You stop building and start juggling.

But the human brain was never meant to operate at the speed of a spreadsheet.

Real efficiency isn't just about getting more things done. It's about getting the *right* things done with the *right kind* of attention. And that kind of work, the deep kind, the kind that moves something inside you or someone else, can't be rushed. It needs time. Stillness. Slowness. Room to breathe.

The best work I've ever done didn't happen during a sprint. It happened when I got quiet enough to think deeply, when I walked away from the screen to let an idea simmer. When I gave myself the unpressured space to explore something before it had a name, that's not inefficiency, that's *craft*.

But our systems aren't built for craft. They're built for throughput. They measure how quickly we respond, how often we show up, and how many hours we log. They track activity, not insight. Responsiveness, not originality.

So we respond. And respond. And respond.

And slowly, the part of us that used to think deeply… forgets how.

We scroll instead of reflect. We reply instead of considering. We publish before we pause.

And we call it efficient.

We've been sold the idea that the faster we go, the more we'll accomplish. But the truth is, we've become faster *at doing less that matters*. We're sprinting across shallow ground, never staying long enough to let anything meaningful take root.

And here's the quiet tragedy: most of us know it.

We feel it in the fatigue that no amount of sleep fixes. In the disconnection from our thoughts. In the nagging sense that we're always behind, even when we're technically ahead.

That's not a time problem. It's a deep problem.

We don't need to become more efficient. We need to become more *present*.

Because the real value of your time isn't in how fast you spend it, it's in what you *give it to*.

And the things that matter most, relationships, ideas, creativity, and change, don't respond to speed. They respond to care. And care can't be rushed.

Efficiency, as we've defined it, is a shallow god.

It gets you through your to-do list.

But it will never get you to the life you want.

# Chapter 5: Designed to Distract

You were never supposed to win this fight.

That tug you feel every time you hear a notification, the reflex to check your phone in line at the grocery store, the impulse to scroll while watching a show, while listening to music, while doing nothing at all, that's not weakness. That's design. And it's working precisely as intended.

The truth is, your phone isn't just a tool. It's a slot machine engineered to keep you pulling the lever.

When we talk about distraction, we usually frame it as a personal failure. We say things like, *I have no self-control,* or *I get so easily distracted.* But distraction in the modern world isn't just a temptation; it's a business model. The companies building our digital environments have one product to sell: **your attention**. And they are very, very good at selling it.

Every ping, badge, buzz, and notification light is a carefully tested psychological trigger. Developers test different shades of red to see which one makes your brain twitch harder. They experiment with vibration patterns and sound cues, mimicking the unpredictable timing of a casino. Why? Because unpredictability keeps you hooked. It activates the brain's reward center more intensely than predictable rewards.

This is the principle of **variable reinforcement**, one of the most potent psychological hooks ever discovered.

Rats in Skinner boxes would press a lever more obsessively when the food pellet came at random intervals, not fixed ones. We're not rats, but we have the same neurological wiring. Every time you refresh your feed, you're gambling. Maybe this time there will be something good. A like. A message. Something new. Something rewarding. The uncertainty is what keeps you coming back.

And when you come back, you're not just consuming, you're being tracked. Every action feeds the algorithm. Every swipe, click, pause, and reaction is data. That data is used to feed you more of what keeps you on the platform, which means more time, more attention, more exposure to ads. You are not the customer. You are the product.

Let that sink in: billions of dollars are spent annually to ensure you do not spend your time the way you want to.

Of course, you feel scattered. Of course, your mind tends to wander. You live in an environment that is intentionally designed to fragment it.

We don't blame fish for swimming when they're in water. Yet we blame ourselves for being distracted when we live inside machines designed to break our focus.

And it goes beyond apps. Your entire digital environment is curated to keep you in motion. Autoplay ensures you don't stop. Infinite scroll means you never reach an end. News alerts demand constant vigilance. Email replaces completion with an unending drip of requests. We are surrounded by systems designed not to inform, but to engage. Not to serve, but to seduce.

Even the language gives it away: *capture attention, retain users, drive engagement*. These are not words of service. They're words of conquest.

And the worst part? We've normalized it. We joke about screen time as if it were an unchangeable law of nature. We speak about our phones like we're in abusive relationships; we can't leave. We accept distraction as the price of admission for modern life.

But that price is high.

It costs us presence. It costs us clarity. It costs us the ability to hear our thoughts without them being shaped by a trending headline or a targeted suggestion.

You cannot do deep work in an environment designed for shallow engagement.

This is not to say you should abandon your devices or swear off social media. This isn't a call to become a monk. It's a call to see clearly. To recognize that the fight for your attention isn't neutral. To understand that distraction isn't just annoying, it's *profitable* for someone else. And until you reclaim control over what enters your mind, someone else will always be programming your mental habits.

Reclaiming your attention doesn't start with more willpower.

It starts with a better design.

You can't always trust yourself to make the best decision in the moment, but you can trust yourself to create an environment that makes those decisions easier. Remove triggers. Disable notifications. Delete the apps that turn you into a consumer of noise. Schedule time to use your devices instead of living inside them by default. These aren't acts of self-denial. They are acts of *self-respect*.

Distraction is not just something that happens to you.

It's something being sold to you.

The question is no longer, *Why can't I focus?*

The question is, who profits when I don't?

# Chapter 6: The Illusion of Input

We consume more information in a day than most people consumed in a year just a century ago.

We listen to podcasts while doing dishes, scroll through news between meetings, check notifications during meals, and binge videos before bed. We follow dozens of thought leaders, subscribe to newsletters, save posts for "later" reading that rarely comes. We are surrounded by words, by content, by input.

And still, we feel behind.

Still, we feel like we haven't done enough.

Still, we wonder why we can't think, why our best ideas feel thin and scattered, why our creativity dries up right when we need it most.

This is the paradox: the more information we take in, the less we seem to retain. The more we consume, the less we digest. We believe we're learning, growing, and getting smarter. But most of the time, we're just filling ourselves without absorbing anything real.

We mistake input for progress.

We scroll through articles and call it research. We hop between hot takes and call it perspective. We bookmark resources we never revisit, listen to hours of ideas we never use, and convince ourselves we're getting ahead because we're surrounded by motion.

But input is not learning. Input is not growth. Input is *potential*. And without time, space, and focused reflection, that potential never becomes anything real.

Think about it: when was the last time you sat with something you read? Not skimmed, not saved, not half-listened to, but *sat with*. When was the last time you reread a paragraph because it sparked something in you? When was the last time an idea from a podcast shaped a real decision you made?

We don't just need less noise, we need more *integration*.

In an age of constant consumption, thinking has become a lost art. We devour information but never metabolize it. We feed our brains and starve our minds. And like the body, the mind cannot thrive on empty calories.

Information has become entertainment.

Learning has become grazing.

We've become connoisseurs of content without letting anything change us.

This is especially dangerous for people who *love* ideas, like you, who likely value growth, knowledge, and perspective. The temptation is to keep taking in more. To treat inspiration as accumulation. To hoard thoughts like we're preparing for a famine that never ends. But the hoarding becomes a habit. And that habit becomes a block.

More input isn't always the answer.

Sometimes it's the obstacle.

Here's what we forget: every new piece of information takes up cognitive space. Your working memory is finite. It's like a whiteboard. If it's already full, writing something new means erasing something old, or cramming the new thought into a corner where you won't see it again. And unlike computers, we can't endlessly "open new tabs" in our minds without slowing the whole system down.

You don't need more tabs.

You need time to process what's already open.

The most effective people I know don't constantly consume. They pause. They reflect. They re-read. They create margin. They let their ideas marinate. And most importantly, they put the input to work by making something with it. A decision. A sentence. A conversation. A shift in direction.

Because until you *use* what you've consumed, it's not yours.

You haven't learned it. You've just passed it through.

It's tempting to think the solution is to unplug entirely, to do a digital detox, to step away from the stream. That can help. But more important than escaping the noise is learning how to *filter* it. To choose input that serves your purpose. To give your brain the space to absorb what it receives. To be intentional with what you allow in, because your mind will eventually reflect what it's full of.

Information is only powerful when it's metabolized.

When it shapes your action.

When it sharpens your insight.

When it deepens your understanding.

You don't need more input. You need more *insight*.

And insight doesn't come from the following article, the next scroll, the next podcast.

It comes from choosing less, sitting longer, and letting the good stuff sink in.

# Chapter 7: The Myth of Urgency

There's a quiet panic built into modern life.

It's not the kind that screams. It hums. A low-grade, constant sense that something is about to slip. A message that needs replying to. A deadline moved up. A notification is waiting. A box is unchecked—something just slightly out of reach. We live with this buzz beneath our skin, a tension we've normalized. And we've learned to call it urgency.

But most of what feels urgent… isn't.

False alarms plague the modern world. A Slack message marked "ASAP" that could've waited until tomorrow. A red badge in your inbox because an automated email from a no-reply address slipped through. A "critical" meeting that was moved up spent 45 minutes circling nothing. And we, trying to be responsible, show up to all of it.

We respond fast because we're told it matters. We feel needed, responsive, on top of things. We associate urgency with value. And so we train ourselves to react quickly, to answer the buzz, to check the notification, to move the task forward, no matter how trivial. We've built systems of speed, not systems of meaning.

But in all this rushing, we rarely stop to ask: *Is this important?*

Urgency, when unchecked, becomes a parasite. It feeds on your attention, your energy, your sense of control. It doesn't need truth to survive, just your reaction. The more you respond, the more it grows. The more you reward it, the more it becomes your default pace. Until eventually, everything feels like a fire to put out, even when nothing's burning.

And here's the cost: when everything feels urgent, nothing is sacred.

Not your thinking time. Not your creativity. Not your evenings. Not your mornings. You give away your best attention to the loudest voice, not the deepest work. You become a firefighter, not a builder. You live in defence, not design.

Urgency tricks you into reacting instead of choosing.

It rewires your brain to prioritize speed over clarity, responsiveness over impact. And over time, it makes you allergic to stillness. You feel anxious when you're not "on," guilty when you're not replying quickly, behind when you take time to think. Rest feels irresponsible. Quiet feels risky.

But let's be clear: most things can wait.

Emails do not expire. Texts do not dissolve. Most decisions don't crumble if you take a breath. The idea that *everything* is time-sensitive is a cultural delusion, a leftover from industries built on machinery and output, not on thought and insight. And it's reinforced by platforms that profit when you're constantly checking in.

The truth is, urgency is often just poor planning, yours or someone else's.

Or it's a lack of boundaries dressed up as importance.

Or it's ego, the belief that you must be in constant motion to matter.

You don't.

The people doing the most impactful work I know don't move fast. They move *intentionally*. They pause. They reflect. They question the timeline before they jump into it. They choose clarity over chaos. They prioritize *what* matters, not just *what screams the loudest*.

You can, too.

This doesn't mean ignoring real emergencies. Of course not. Life has those moments, and we rise to meet them. But most "urgencies" in your inbox aren't emergencies; they're just someone else's anxiety arriving on your screen. You are not obligated to absorb it.

What if urgency wasn't your default?

What if you asked yourself, before responding: Is this significant right now? Is this the best use of my clearest mind? My best hour?

You might find that much of what you thought required immediate attention… doesn't require you at all.

You might find that time expands when you stop sprinting toward nothing.

Urgency will always exist in the world. But it doesn't have to live in you.

You don't owe your speed to anyone.

You owe your attention to what matters.

# Chapter 8: The Cognitive Toll

There's a moment, late in the day, when you stare at your screen and realize you've been rereading the same sentence for five minutes. Your eyes move across the words, but your mind slides off them like glass water. You try again, slower this time, but the focus won't come. It's like your brain is fogged over. Not tired in the physical sense. Just… dulled. Clouded. Flat.

That feeling isn't laziness. It's cognitive fatigue.

And it's one of the hidden costs of living in a multitasking world.

We often treat our brains like limitless machines. If we're not lifting heavy things or sweating, we assume we haven't "used up" any real energy. But mental energy is just as real, and just as exhaustible, as physical stamina. And multitasking, despite its reputation for productivity, is one of the most draining things you can ask your brain to do.

Let's get clear on something: **your brain can't multitask.** Not in the way we use the word.

What we call multitasking is *task switching, which involves* rushing between different cognitive demands. And every switch has a cost. A hidden, invisible toll that chips away at your clarity, memory, and decision-making.

When you switch from writing an email to checking a text to jumping back into a spreadsheet, your brain doesn't flip seamlessly from one lane to another. It has to disengage from the mental model of one task and reload the context of the next. This switching process, known as attention residue, means that part of your brain remains stuck in the previous task even as you try to engage with the new one.

That's why after a few switches; your thinking becomes fuzzy. You can't remember what you just read. You lose track of details. You start rereading, second-guessing, and overlooking.

It's not that you've lost your intelligence.

It's because you've burned your bandwidth.

In one well-known study by the American Psychological Association, researchers found that frequent multitaskers performed worse on cognitive control tasks than those who preferred to do one thing at a time. They were more easily distracted, slower to switch between tasks, and less able to filter out irrelevant information.

Even more surprising? People who believed they were *good* at multitasking turned out to be the *worst* at it.

It's like a mental hangover we've all learned to live with. But the effects compound over time.

When you spend all day switching tasks, you don't just get tired. You get shallow.

Your thoughts don't run as deep. Your ideas don't connect as easily. Your creativity dries up. You might check off more boxes, but you make more mistakes, miss more nuance, and struggle to hold complex ideas in your head.

And this isn't just about work. It affects your life in subtle but powerful ways.

You forget appointments. Misplace things. Leave a conversation feeling like you weren't fully present. Snap at someone not because you're angry, but because your mind is stretched too thin to respond with patience. You start to feel like you're constantly behind, even when you've been "busy" all day.

This is the cumulative effect of a taxed mind.

And the world is designed to ignore it.

Because we reward performance, not presence. We reward visibility, not depth. We measure how fast people respond, not how they think. And in that rush, we quietly degrade the very tools we need to create meaningful work and meaningful lives: focus, memory, insight, and patience.

The irony is that we think multitasking will help us get more done. But what it does is slowly *erode our ability to think well at all.*

So, if you've felt foggy lately, forgetful, distracted, dulled, don't blame your intelligence. Blame the toll. Your brain isn't broken. It's overworked.

And the answer isn't to push harder. It's too slow for your mind to recover.

Because clarity isn't just a nice-to-have.

It's your best resource.

And it can only exist when you protect it from the cost of doing too much, too fast, all the time.

# Chapter 9: Emotional Fragmentation

You're in the middle of a conversation, but you're also thinking about the email you haven't answered. Your phone buzzes. You glance at it. You nod at the person in front of you, pretending to listen, while mentally switching tabs to tomorrow's meeting. You smile, offer a generic response, and walk away feeling vaguely disconnected, like you were there, but not really.

This isn't just a distraction.

This is emotional fragmentation.

We usually talk about multitasking as a productivity issue—a matter of time, efficiency, maybe mental focus. But the deeper cost is emotional. When your attention is split, your presence is split. And when your presence is split, so is your ability to feel fully.

Multitasking doesn't just weaken your focus. It fragments your humanity.

The human brain and heart were designed for coherence. For wholeness. For living in one moment at a time, with one set of emotions, one channel of connection. But in the age of fractured attention, we're asked to feel multiple things at once, across various contexts, constantly.

We move from a serious news headline to a joke to a calendar invite to a tragic story to a meme to a photo of someone's wedding, all within minutes. And then we're expected to return to work, to parent, to plan dinner, to reply to that text. Our emotional states are constantly being stirred, redirected, and blurred.

We scroll through a feed and pass through a dozen emotional climates. Concern, envy, excitement, outrage, guilt, curiosity, numbness. No time to process. No time to settle. We keep scrolling. Keep switching. Keep absorbing.

Eventually, we feel everything at once, but nothing fully.

This is emotional multitasking: the simultaneous juggling of input, performance, and response without any one feeling being allowed to land completely. And over time, this fragments us. We begin to lose clarity about how we feel. We struggle to access absolute joy. Or deep grief. Or true calm. Everything feels dulled, flattened, skimmed.

We become emotionally overstimulated but undernourished.

And it starts to show in our relationships. We get snappier, less patient. We listen half-heartedly. We zone out in the middle of a story. Not because we don't care, but because our bandwidth is gone. We can't offer presence because we don't have any left to give. The people we love feel it. So do we.

It also shows up in decision-making. When you're emotionally fragmented, your intuition becomes foggy. You second-guess yourself. You make reactive choices instead of reflective ones. You agree to things you shouldn't, delay stuff you need to face, and tell yourself you're just "too tired to think clearly." And maybe you are, because thinking requires *feeling* first.

But clarity can't grow in a fragmented mind.

The more our attention becomes split, the more we lose access to that inner compass, what matters, what we care about, what's enough. Instead, we substitute quick reactions for slow understanding. We rush to keep up with emotional demands instead of sitting with what we truly feel.

Here's the cost no one talks about: multitasking makes you emotionally thin.

It takes the richness of human experience and chops it into digestible fragments. It teaches us to avoid discomfort by switching tasks. To bypass hard conversations with screen time. To scroll through sadness instead of facing it. To skim the surface of joy instead of soaking in it. And over time, we start to believe that's all life is: fragments.

But it's not.

You're not supposed to feel everything at once. You're supposed to feel one thing at a time. To let joy fill you when it comes. To let sadness take its time. To listen with your whole self. To cry without checking your calendar. To laugh without checking your phone. To be there, not just with your body, but with your mind, your heart, your breath.

Emotional wholeness can't coexist with constant switching.

And the good news is, the first step back to wholeness isn't complicated.

It starts with presence.

With choosing one thing to feel, one person to be with, one moment to inhabit. Silencing the pings. By letting your attention settle in one place long enough for your emotions to catch up.

Because when you allow yourself to feel fully, you start to live fully again.

And that's not a productivity upgrade.

That's a return to being human.

# Chapter 10: When Everything Is a Tab, Nothing Is a Page

There's a unique kind of fatigue that comes from having twenty things halfway done and none entirely held.

It's not physical tiredness. It's not even stress in the traditional sense. It's a kind of quiet mental erosion. The reason that your thoughts are thin, your attention is diluted, and your presence is always just a few degrees out of focus. That feeling? That's what happens when your life becomes a series of tabs, open, overlapping, and mostly unattended.

We've been trained to live like browsers.

Each conversation, project, relationship, and moment is treated like a tab. We click between them constantly. Half-thoughts in one. Unanswered messages in another. Tasks we'll "get back to later." Emotional residue from the last thing, bleeding into the next.

And just like a computer, our minds slow down under the weight of all that fragmentation.

You know the moment. Too many tabs open, the fan in your laptop kicks on, and the screen starts to lag. Nothing crashes outright, but everything slows. That's your brain, too. Always on, constantly flickering, always partially loaded but never fully committed. You start things but don't finish them. You engage but don't connect. You respond but don't reflect.

And slowly, without realizing it, you stop reading your own life like a page.

Because a page is different from a tab.

A page holds your attention. It asks you to move through it slowly, line by line. It has structure. Sequence. Context. Meaning builds as you go. When you live like a page, you can feel where you are. You're grounded in a story, not lost in a storm.

But we've replaced pages with tabs. We've made every part of life skimmable.

Relationships become message threads. Creativity becomes "content." Even memory becomes scattered, a photo here, a calendar event there, a note saved in an app you forgot you had. We've outsourced continuity. We tell ourselves we'll return to these open tabs. But often, we don't. And the fragments pile up. We carry the weight of unresolved issues.

Worse still, we've normalized this pace.

We expect to feel distracted. We hope to forget things. We aim to seamlessly transition between screens, apps, and conversations without compromising quality. But we are losing something. And it's not just productivity.

We're losing *coherence*.

When your life is all tabs, you forget what it feels like to be immersed. To be all in. To give your full presence to one person, one task, one idea. You stop remembering how it feels to lose track of time doing something meaningful. To hear yourself think. To start something and see it through, not just to completion, but to understanding.

You begin to confuse motion with progress.

And you begin to forget what focus feels like, how peaceful it is, how quiet, how rich.

Here's what no one tells you: multitasking doesn't just affect your performance.

It rewires your sense of time.

You stop experiencing your days as stories and start experiencing them as stacks—a vertical pile of unfinished things. You don't turn pages. You click between windows. You don't move through moments; you glance off them.

Eventually, it all starts to feel the same. Urgent. Surface-level. Forgettable.

But you were not built to live a life of tabs.

You were built to inhabit your days with intention.

You were built to *read* the story of your own life, not just skim it.

So close, a few. Let the unnecessary ones go. Finish the ones that matter. Leave space for what's next. Not everything needs to stay open. Not everything deserves your bandwidth.

Because when everything is a tab, nothing is a page.

And without pages, you'll never feel like you're inside your life; you'll always feel like you're circling it.

# Part II: The Roots of Real Focus

## Chapter 11: Attention Is the Beginning of Devotion

Years ago, I came across a line by the poet Mary Oliver that stopped me cold: *"Attention is the beginning of devotion."* I didn't fully understand it then. It sounded beautiful, sure, lyrical, profound, but abstract. Attention as devotion? What did that mean? I only began to grasp it when I started to lose both.

There was a period in my life when everything felt urgent and nothing felt real. I would be talking to someone I loved while simultaneously glancing at my phone. I would be eating dinner while mentally drafting tomorrow's presentation. I would go for a walk and reach the end of it without remembering the trees I passed, the air I breathed, the way my body had even moved.

I was present everywhere, and yet nowhere.

And when I finally slowed down, intentionally, with discomfort, I noticed something I hadn't felt in a long time. A strange ache, like a muscle that hadn't been used. It wasn't just my capacity for focus that had atrophied. It was my capacity for *devotion* to people, to purpose, to the moment in front of me.

I had been living distractedly for so long that I forgot that real attention is an act of love.

You don't need to be a mystic to feel this. You've felt it when someone listens to you without interrupting. When a friend notices the tremor in your voice before you say you're not okay. When a child looks at you with full concentration, waiting for your answer as if it's the most essential thing in the world. That's not just attention. That's devotion. Its presence is given freely, without demand, without hurry.

And it's disappearing.

Not because we don't care, but because we don't slow down long enough to show that we do.

Attention has been reduced to a commodity. We discuss it in terms of metrics, including average view time, open rates, impressions, and bounce rates. We've begun to believe that all attention is equal, that a glance is the same as a gaze. That presence is measured in clicks. That attention is something we *take*, not something we *offer*.

But that's not true.

Real attention is not passive. It's not just noticing. It's choosing to *stay*. To remain with something long enough for it to change you.

When you give something your full attention, you begin to care about it more deeply. And the reverse is true, too: the more you care about something, the more you're willing to give it your attention. That's why Oliver's line lands with such power. Attention and devotion aren't separate. They are the same act, seen from different sides.

This is why multitasking feels so empty over time. It divides not only your focus, but your care. You cannot be fully with something if you are partially with everything. And the cost of this isn't just cognitive. It's spiritual. When you live in a state of constant partial attention, you begin to lose your sense of intimacy with life itself.

I'm not just talking about romantic intimacy or emotional connection. I'm talking about the simple, sacred act of being with something long enough to know it. To understand it. To let it show you something.

It might be a project. It might be a piece of music. It might be your thoughts. It might be someone you see every day but rarely *see*. Whatever it is, it requires what we've forgotten how to give: undivided presence.

We used to focus on fewer things, and we gave our attention more freely. Now, we divide it into digital confetti and scatter it across the landscape of our lives. And then we wonder why things don't feel meaningful anymore. It's not because life has gotten smaller. It's because our focus has gotten thinner.

Meaning grows where attention goes.

And attention, like love, requires effort. It is an act of will. Not willpower in the punitive sense, but the will to slow down, to choose depth, to return when distraction pulls you away. It is not about perfection, it's about presence.

There is nothing inherently noble about being productive. There is something deeply noble, however, about being present. Because presence is what allows you to encounter your life fully, and that encounter, when sustained, is what becomes devotion.

We all want to live intensely. To love fully. To do work that matters. But none of those things happen in fragments. They require attention. Not the kind you give while multitasking, nodding, half-hearing. The kind that shows up and stays.

That's what makes attention sacred. It says: *I see you. I choose you. I am here.*

And when you offer that to the world, the world offers
something back.

Not in likes. Not in stats.

In meaning.

In depth.

In devotion.

# Chapter 12: The Brain Isn't Built for Multitasking

We think we're good at it.

Sending an email while listening to a podcast, scanning a text during a meeting, and watching a video while replying to comments. We convince ourselves that multitasking makes us more efficient. That we're just wired that way. That we can handle it.

But here's the uncomfortable truth: you are not multitasking. You are switching tasks rapidly. And every switch comes at a cost.

Your brain isn't a factory line with separate departments humming along in parallel. It's more like a spotlight in a dark room, capable of illuminating one object at a time. You can move that spotlight quickly from one task to another, but you can't shine it in two places with equal clarity. When you try, you don't split focus, you fracture it.

Cognitive science has a term for this: **task-switching cost**. It refers to the mental lag, the lost processing power, and the increased error rate that comes from toggling between tasks. Even seemingly small switches, such as glancing at a notification or answering a quick message, disrupt the neural patterns your brain has built around the task at hand.

Imagine trying to write a story, and every few sentences, someone whispers a riddle in your ear. Even if you answer quickly, it takes time to find your place again in the narrative. That's your brain trying to reestablish *context*. It's not just about remembering what you were doing. It's about rebuilding the mental framework, the connections, associations, and short-term memory loops that support deep thinking.

The more you switch, the harder this becomes. The spotlight grows dimmer. The connections grow weaker. And the work, even if finished, lacks depth.

Multiple studies confirm this. In experiments where participants were asked to alternate between tasks, performance consistently dropped. Tasks took longer. Mistakes increased. Memory retention declined. What's more, people *felt* like they were being productive, even as their output deteriorated.

That last point is crucial. Multitasking creates a sense of busy effort, which we often confuse with real productivity. But movement is not the same as momentum. A bouncing mind is not a focused mind. And the feeling of doing many things at once often masks the reality that you're not doing any of them well.

This isn't a flaw. It's biology.

Your prefrontal cortex, the part of your brain responsible for attention, planning, and decision-making, is optimized for *sequencing*, not parallel processing. It's designed to engage deeply with a single complex task, to hold relevant details in working memory, and to make adjustments as needed. But when you overload it, it starts to fail in subtle ways.

You forgot why you opened that tab.

You reread the same sentence twice.

You walk into a room and can't remember why.

None of these moments means you're broken. They tell you you're over-switched.

And the toll is cumulative. The more your brain adapts to rapid switching, the less comfortable it becomes with sustained attention. This is why, over time, it gets harder to read a book without checking your phone. Harder to sit through a quiet moment without reaching for something. Your neural pathways have been rewired to seek novelty, not depth.

It's no accident that social media platforms thrive on this wiring. They give you exactly what your multitasked brain craves: bursts of stimulation, short hits of novelty, a sense of motion with minimal cognitive load. And they make it harder to return to anything that requires actual mental effort.

So, what do we do?

We start by acknowledging reality: the brain isn't made for multitasking. The more we fight this truth, the more we suffer. But when we accept it, we open the door to better design of our days, our habits, our environments.

You don't need to become a monk. But you do need to stop expecting your brain to act like a machine.

Choose one thing at a time.

Give it more than a sliver of yourself.

Let your spotlight focus on something long enough for it to matter.

That's not inefficiency.

That's intelligence, working the way it was built to work.

And it's the only way to do work that lasts.

# Chapter 13: Switching Costs: The Hidden Drain

It always seems harmless. Just a quick reply. A glance at a notification. A quick check of the inbox, followed by a quick scroll while waiting for a document to load. We tell ourselves it's fine that it won't take long. That we'll get right back to what we were doing.

And maybe we do. But we don't return the same.

Because every time you switch tasks, no matter how small, you leave behind a little of your focus, and you carry a little of the distraction with you.

That's the hidden cost.

Cognitive scientists call this **switching cost**, the subtle, compounding mental toll of interrupting your attention and then trying to redirect it. It's not the time spent on the side task that does the damage. It's the residue it leaves behind.

When you're in deep focus, your brain is in what's called a "task-set", a tightly wired network of short-term memory, rules, priorities, and sensory filters that support what you're doing. It's the reason you can write a paragraph and hold the structure of a sentence while forming the next one. It's how you keep multiple steps of a plan in mind while executing one of them.

But every time you switch, your brain has to disassemble that task set and build a new one from scratch. And that process takes time. Not a lot, usually just seconds, but it adds up, especially when it happens dozens or even hundreds of times a day.

If you've ever wondered why a full day of "small tasks" can leave you more exhausted than a day of concentrated work, this is why. You're not just using your time; you're burning your mental fuel in inefficient loops. The transitions are what drain you, not just the work.

Worse, those transitions often go unnoticed. You think you're managing fine. You don't feel the cost right away. But later, when you find yourself staring blankly at a screen, struggling to find words, missing obvious steps, that's the lag catching up with you.

It's like compound interest, but in reverse.

And it doesn't stop at fatigue. Switching costs erode accuracy, memory, and quality. Studies have shown that frequent task-switchers make more mistakes and are slower overall than those who focus on one task at a time, even when the multitaskers think they're moving faster. This dissonance, between how busy we *feel* and how well we perform, is one of the quiet tragedies of modern work.

And it's not just about your job. The cost shows up in your relationships, too.

You switch from a conversation to a notification and back again, thinking you haven't missed anything. But you have. Tone, nuance, emotion. The unsaid things that only emerge when you're fully attuned to someone. You can nod and smile, but they feel your partial presence. Your divided attention. And slowly, subtly, trust erodes.

You also lose connection to yourself.

Try journaling, meditating, or sitting with a tricky question in your life. The moment you break that concentration, even for a second, the thread snaps. The insight fades. The emotional depth disappears. Not because it wasn't real, but because your mind was pulled out of the state required to meet it.

We treat interruptions like temporary diversions.

But they change the *quality* of what we return to.

And here's the insidious part: our environments are designed to maximize these switches. Open office plans. Phones within arm's reach. Tabs piled up. Notifications defaulted to "on." We are surrounded by frictionless access to distraction, yet we're surprised when our minds feel scattered.

The answer isn't to have superhuman discipline.

It's to reduce the number of times your brain has to reload itself.

One task. One window. One block of time. It's not always possible, but it has more potential than we think.

Because every time you protect your focus, you reclaim energy you would've lost to switching.

You preserve the thread. You deepen the groove. You give your brain a chance to settle into the state where absolute clarity and creativity live.

The cost of switching is hidden. But the reward of staying with one thing?

That's when everything changes.

# Chapter 14: Flow and the Human Machine

There's a rhythm your brain is always looking for. A sweet spot. Not too hard, not too easy. Not so dull that you want to escape, and not so overwhelming that you freeze. Just the right amount of challenge, just the right amount of skill. When you find it, time warps. Distractions fall away. Action and awareness merge. You lose your sense of self, not in a numb, detached way, but in the best way possible.

This is **flow**, and it is the opposite of multitasking.

Psychologist Mihaly Csikszentmihalyi spent decades studying this state. He wasn't interested in productivity hacks or motivational speeches. He wanted to understand why some people seemed to experience deep joy and meaning in their work, their play, their lives. What he found was that the most fulfilling moments weren't passive. They weren't about relaxation or escape. They were about *full engagement*.

Flow happens when you're doing something that fully absorbs you. It could be writing, painting, solving a problem, or building something with your hands. It could be in a conversation, a game, a run, or a prayer. The setting doesn't matter. What matters is an *undivided presence*.

And that's why multitasking kills flow before it even begins.

You cannot enter a flow state while switching tasks. The mind needs time, real, uninterrupted time, to settle into focus. To establish the proper levels of concentration, dopamine, and feedback. When we interrupt that process, even with a glance or a micro-decision, we reset the clock.

Flow isn't a trick you can turn on at will. It's a *consequence* of continuity.

You have to earn it. You have to stay.

What's wild is that flow is often the very thing people are trying to access when they multitask. They want momentum. They want energy. They want the satisfaction of progress. But they chase it in fragments, jumping between tasks, feeding themselves little bits of dopamine from emails, updates, and quick wins. And then they wonder why it feels like nothing ever lands.

Here's what we forget: the human brain is a slow-starting machine.

It takes time to gather itself. To move from surface-level awareness to deep, immersive thinking. To link ideas, to build context, to start solving problems in a nonlinear way. That's where flow lives. Not in the first five minutes. In the fifteenth. Or the thirtieth. Or the hour you didn't think you had.

But we rarely give ourselves that chance.

We check our phones during breaks instead of letting our minds wander. We interrupt creative work to answer quick questions. We fill every moment of stillness with stimulation. And in doing so, we short-circuit the only process that leads to the clarity we crave.

You don't need to work harder. You need to *stay longer*.

Not at your desk. Not at your job. In your mind. In the process. In the discomfort of staying with something that doesn't immediately reward you.

Because when you stay, something extraordinary happens. The task stops feeling like effort. You stop monitoring yourself.

The world narrows. You become absorbed. You begin to forget time. And what you're doing becomes not just productive, but meaningful.

That's not magic. That's flow. That's how the machine of your brain was meant to operate.

And once you've felt it, you realize how shallow most of our daily multitasking is.

You realize you no longer want to live with one foot in and one foot out. You want to do one thing well. You want to get inside the work. You want to experience life from the inside out, not just observe it through the noise.

Flow doesn't require you to be brilliant.

It just requires you to be *there*.

Not glancing and not switching. Not half-in, half-out.

Fully in.

That's where real momentum begins.

# Chapter 15: Your Brain on Deep Work

There's a kind of silence that settles in when you've been focused long enough. Not the silence of your surroundings, those might still be full of noise, but the silence inside. The chatter dies down. The pull to check something fades. You're not resisting distractions because they're no longer present. You're immersed. You're doing the work, and the work is doing something to you.

This is what happens when your brain enters a state of deep work.

It's not just a mental posture. It's a neurological event. Functional MRI scans show that during deep focus, the prefrontal cortex, the area responsible for decision-making, attention, and goal-setting, lights up in sustained patterns. Your brain waves shift, your working memory sharpens, and your sense of self starts to recede just slightly, making room for the task itself to take center stage.

The more time you spend in this state, the more efficient your brain becomes at forming new connections. You're not just doing better work, you're getting smarter while doing it.

That's something we rarely acknowledge. We tend to think of focus as a discipline issue, something that serves productivity. But deep work doesn't just help you get more done. It builds mental strength. It strengthens your capacity to think abstractly, to problem-solve in novel ways, and to retain complex ideas over time.

The process isn't flashy. It's often slow and quiet. It might begin with some resistance, your brain trying to pull you back to the surface, but if you stay, you cross a threshold. You stop scanning for new stimuli. You stop wondering what else is happening. Your working memory stops juggling loose threads. It starts organizing. Pattern recognition improves. Ideas connect more naturally. You begin to make intuitive leaps, not because of inspiration, but because you've cleared the space for them to land.

And here's where the real difference emerges: deep work leads to insight.

Not just output, but understanding. Not just quantity, but clarity.

This is what makes it radically different from the multitasking model of getting through a checklist. Multitasking keeps you in a reactive loop. You're constantly responding, constantly moving forward, but never downward, never into the core of what something means or why it matters.

Deep work, on the other hand, invites depth by its very nature. It forces you to choose. To block out everything else and say, "This is what I'm doing. Nothing else." That simple act of commitment reshapes your cognitive architecture. It reorients your values, your momentum, and, over time, your identity.

Of course, the world doesn't make this easy. Most environments aren't built for deep work. Interruptions are treated as usual. Slack messages, pings, emails, alerts, they feel small, but they fracture the focus you've worked hard to build. The effort it takes to re-enter deep focus after an interruption can be significant. One moment of reactivity can erase thirty minutes of mental buildup.

That's why deep work requires protection. It doesn't happen by accident. It has to be designed, defended, and respected. And that's not about being rigid or elitist about your time. It's about understanding what your mind needs to function at its highest level and refusing to trade that capacity for the short-term sugar rush of minor tasks.

Sometimes people assume deep work must be complicated. It requires a dramatic ritual or perfect conditions. But it can begin with something as small as a time block. A single hour where the phone is off, the door is closed, and the work gets your full attention. In that hour, you might produce less in terms of raw quantity than during a multitasked sprint, but the quality, and more importantly, the *insight*, will far outweigh it.

Your brain was built to go deep. It's weird to crave it, even if it takes effort to get there. And once you experience that state with regularity, your tolerance for distraction begins to shrink. You notice how shallow most digital noise is. You become less reactive, more reflective. You start to structure your day differently, not because someone told you to, but because you remember what it feels like to think clearly, and you want that back.

That clarity isn't just for creatives or thinkers or academics. It's for anyone who wants to live deliberately. Who wants their hours to count for something more than just responsiveness? Who wants to spend time *inside* the work, not just hovering above it?

We all have access to that space.

But it begins by doing the thing we've been trained to avoid, staying with one thought long enough to watch it unfold.

# Chapter 16: How We Learned to Fragment

This didn't start with the smartphone.

The habit of splitting our attention, of doing many things poorly instead of one thing well, goes back much further. It's easy to blame modern tech for our fractured minds, and in some ways, that blame is justified. But the foundation was laid long before apps, notifications, and dopamine-driven platforms ever entered the picture. We were taught to fragment. We were conditioned into it, slowly, subtly, and systemically.

For most of human history, attention was survival. To be distracted was to be vulnerable. We evolved to be sensitive to shifts in our environment, to movement, to sound, to change. That sensitivity served us. But in the last two centuries, the world changed faster than our minds could adapt.

The Industrial Revolution introduced machines, and with them, the idea that people, too, could become more efficient. Work shifted from rhythm-based labor, like farming or craftsmanship, to mechanized repetition. It wasn't about mastery anymore; it was about throughput. You weren't paid to think; you were paid to perform a task, as fast and as consistently as possible.

Time became a metric. Hours, output, shifts. This was the beginning of the external schedule overtaking the internal one. And it planted the idea that the more tasks you could handle, the more valuable you were. The mind was no longer something to cultivate. It was something to maximize.

That mindset expanded with the growth of corporate culture. Productivity wasn't just a professional virtue; it became a personal one. People began measuring their worth not by how they lived, but by how much they could produce. "Hardworking" became a compliment. "Busy" became a badge. Slowness became suspect.

Then came the digital age. At first, the promise was freedom. Faster communication meant more time, right? Less friction, fewer barriers. And for a moment, it seemed genuine. Emails replaced memos. Meetings moved online. Tasks that once took days were done in minutes. But the speed didn't slow us down. It made us hungrier.

We filled every open moment.

If the internet gave us access to more, we reasoned, then *more* must always be better. More knowledge. More tools. More efficiency. But instead of space and clarity, we got noise and clutter. Instead of using digital tools to deepen our thinking, we started using them to fragment it further. One window became five. Five became twenty. We convinced ourselves we could handle it.

And for a while, we did, until the toll started to show.

By the time smartphones entered our pockets, we were already living fragmented lives. The phone didn't create our scattered minds; it just gave us a way to carry them everywhere.

It's essential to understand this history, not to assign blame, but to recognize that the way we live now was built. Designed. Reinforced. If we learned to live in fragments, then we can also unlearn it. But it means questioning more than our habits. It means asking about the values that shaped them.

Because even today, we're rewarded for juggling. "Multitasking" still appears on résumés as if it were a skill. We praise students who balance clubs, coursework, part-time jobs, and volunteer work, without ever asking if they have time to think deeply about any of it. We design school days in blocks and meetings in half-hours, as if a change of subject every 45 minutes is just how the mind works.

And we carry that expectation into adulthood. Into parenting. Into relationships. We check our phones during dinner and call it "just staying connected." We interrupt tasks because "this will only take a second." We work on ten things in parallel, telling ourselves this is what responsibility looks like.

But it's not a responsibility. It's a reaction.

And it leaves us constantly in motion, but rarely at rest. Updated continuously, but seldom reflective. Surrounded by options, but unclear on what matters.

We were not meant to live this way.

Your brain, the human brain, was made for sustained attention. For following ideas through to the end. For engaging fully with your environment, your work, and your people. The world may have changed, but the architecture of your mind has not. You're still built for depth, not distraction.

That truth has been buried under layers of cultural conditioning. But it's not lost.

You don't need to return to a pre-digital age. You don't need to quit your job, throw away your phone, or escape into the woods. What you need is awareness. Awareness of how we got here. Awareness that what we call normal was a decision made by industries, by systems, by cultural defaults.

And awareness that you can make different decisions.

You can build your life around coherence, not fragmentation. You can rebuild focus, not as a rare state you stumble into, but as a practice you protect. The world taught you to live in fragments. Now it's time to remember how to live whole.

# Chapter 17: Silence Is a Skill

Silence used to be everywhere.

It was part of daily life, between tasks, between conversations, between the sounds of the world. You walked without music. You cooked without podcasts. You sat on a train and looked out the window without a screen to pull your attention elsewhere. Silence wasn't something you had to carve out. It was just there, like air.

Now it's an endangered state.

The moment things go quiet, we reach. For the phone. For the feed. For something, anything, to fill the pause. We've grown uncomfortable with stillness, even allergic to it. And we tell ourselves it's just a matter of preference, how the world works now. But there's something deeper going on.

We've forgotten that silence isn't empty. It's *active*. It's where integration happens. It's where thoughts cohere. It's where emotion catches up with cognition. It's where awareness lives, not the frantic scanning kind, but the full-bodied kind that lets you inhabit your own experience.

That kind of silence doesn't just show up anymore. You have to make space for it. And that's why it's become a skill.

It's not about noise levels. It's about stimulus. About resisting the reflex to fill every in-between moment. About letting the brain settle instead of constantly stirring it with new input. It takes practice to let the silence stretch just a little longer. To sit in it without immediately checking, scrolling, or replying.

We've trained ourselves to believe that every blank space is a productivity problem.

Waiting in line? Scroll.

Walking alone? Call someone.

Sitting at a red light? Tap your screen, check the news.

These aren't huge decisions. They're micro-responses. But they add up to a life with no margins. A life where the mind never breathes, never rests, never listens to itself.

And when silence disappears, so does depth.

Because you need silence to think clearly. Not just to "process", that word we throw around as if thinking is a background app, but to do the real work of inner alignment. Knowing what you believe. Hearing what's beneath your reaction. Feeling the whole shape of a decision before you move.

We don't realize how much we outsource to noise. How often do we fill the silence before something meaningful has a chance to emerge? A realization. A memory. A moment of empathy. Those things don't shout. They wait.

And if you never give them a chance, they never arrive.

Silence also holds something else: repair. The nervous system settles in stillness. Thoughts that were tangled have space to unknot themselves. Emotion, pushed down in the churn of distraction, has room to surface. This is why quiet moments can bring tears without warning. It's not a weakness. It's your inner world catching up to you.

But it's hard. Because silence doesn't flatter us, it doesn't reward us with likes. It doesn't feel productive or measurable. You don't finish a walk in silence and announce how much you've "accomplished." You feel a little more whole. A little more rooted. A little more like yourself.

That's the reward. And it only comes with practice.

Not grand gestures, just small returns. Leaving the phone behind on a walk and sitting in a room without reaching for stimulation, pausing before opening the next app, choosing not to respond immediately, and letting a thought linger.

Silence is not absence. It is presence, stripped of noise.

And learning to sit in it again is not a retreat from the world. It's a way of returning to it, more fully aware, less frayed, more capable of offering what the moment needs.

It's not an escape.

It's a strength.

A practiced stillness that allows you to hold your attention like it matters, because it does.

# Chapter 18: The Role of Boredom

We're terrified of being bored.

It's almost instinctual now, the way our hand reaches for the phone the moment a pause appears. Waiting in line, sitting in traffic, lying in bed before sleep. If there's even a flicker of stillness, we fill it. We don't say we're bored, we say we're "catching up," or "just checking something." But the behaviour is the same: avoid the void.

And it is a void, in a way. Boredom creates space where something used to be. It strips away the stream of stimulation we've become used to. It feels, at first, like emptiness. But if you stay with it, if you don't rush to escape, it becomes something else entirely. It becomes *accessible*.

Boredom, despite its bad reputation, is not a problem. It's a doorway.

It's a signal that your mind is unoccupied. And that unoccupied space? That's where creativity lives. That's where self-awareness surfaces. That's where the scattered parts of your attention begin to gather.

Children instinctively know this. When they get bored, their imagination kicks in. They invent stories, build things, and explore. They don't need constant entertainment to be alive in their minds; they need enough boredom to get started. But even this is changing. Screen time now competes with silence from the moment they can hold a device. And so we see boredom not as an opportunity, but as a threat to be eliminated.

We've carried that same avoidance into adulthood. We use technology not just to fill gaps but to smooth over every wrinkle of waiting, wondering, or wandering. And then we wonder why we can't think deeply, why our best ideas don't arrive, and why we feel disconnected from ourselves. But when would those insights even show up? We never leave the door open long enough for them to enter.

This doesn't mean all boredom is profound. There is a difference between passive boredom, the kind that numbs, and active boredom, the kind that signals a shift. The first can make you listless; the second can make you curious. But the difference depends on what you do with it.

If you run from boredom every time it appears, you'll never reach the second kind. You'll stay in the shallows of distraction, constantly feeding the next urge, never dropping deep enough to see what might unfold.

Boredom is often the beginning of focus, not the enemy of it.

Many people assume the ability to concentrate means forcing the mind to stay engaged. But the opposite is often true. The most productive thinkers, writers, designers, and problem-solvers I know all do something similar: they let themselves be bored. Not indefinitely, but long enough for the noise to fall away. They walk without input. They stare out the windows. They sit in silence and wait.

And somewhere in that waiting, the mind shifts. An idea appears. A thread unravels. A memory rises. Not because they chased it, but because they made space for it.

That's the value of boredom. It gives the brain time to process, to restore, and to reveal what's been simmering beneath the surface. It pulls you out of the rapid-response cycle and back into the slower, more fertile rhythms of reflection and insight.

If you're always entertained, you never get to that part of yourself. You never hear the quieter thoughts. The ones that don't shout for attention but shape the way you see the world.

So, the next time boredom appears, don't swat it away.

Let it stay a little longer than is comfortable. Don't fill the silence immediately. Don't refresh the feed. Don't reach for the podcast just yet.

Let the moment expand.

Let the quiet grow wide enough to show you something you didn't know you were carrying.

That isn't wasted time.

It's the start of real thinking.

# Chapter 19: Rhythm Over Hustle

There's a difference between movement and momentum.

Hustle celebrates movement, fast, relentless, unquestioning. It doesn't ask whether the direction makes sense, only whether you're going hard enough. Hustle says rest is weakness, that stillness is failure, that slowness is for people who don't want it badly enough. It tells you to work until you crash, then drink something caffeinated and get back to it.

But the human mind doesn't thrive on hustle. It thrives on rhythm.

Nature works in rhythms. Our bodies do too. There are cycles woven into the fabric of every living thing, light and dark, inhale and exhale, surge and retreat. Attention follows that same arc. You can't be entirely on all the time. You're not supposed to be. Your brain is wired to work in pulses of intensity followed by recovery.

Push, then pause. Focus, then reset. That's rhythm. And it's how you do your best work without burning out.

The problem is, our culture doesn't honour that pattern. We are expected to be available constantly, responsive instantly, and productive endlessly. We fill every pause. We treat downtime like a flaw in the schedule. We keep adding more and more apps, more alerts, more meetings, hoping to keep the machine running. And for a while, it does.

Until it doesn't.

You know the feeling: the mental flatline at 2 p.m. The fog after too many back-to-back tasks. The difficulty of switching off at night, even though your body is exhausted. These aren't just signs of busyness. They're signs of dissonance, of pushing against the natural rhythm your mind needs to recover.

If your phone overheats, you don't question it. Close the apps, give it space, and let it cool down. But when your brain does the same, you think something's wrong with you. That's the lie of hustle. It treats humans like hardware.

But you are not a machine.

You are a living system, designed to ebb and flow. To work in cycles of 60 to 90 minutes, not all-day marathons. This is something scientists call ultradian rhythms, natural peaks and valleys of alertness throughout the day. Ignoring them wastes energy. Align with them, and your focus sharpens.

Rhythm doesn't mean you work less. It means you work *better*.

It means planning for periods of proper focus, uninterrupted by shallow tasks, and then stepping away before your mind starts to splinter. It means scheduling space between meetings, taking breaks before you think you need them, and building routines that protect your highest-energy hours for your most meaningful work.

This is the opposite of multitasking. It's single-tasking with intention. And it's not just effective, it's sustainable.

But it takes courage.

It takes pushing back on the cultural pressure to always be "on." It takes not apologizing for needing recovery. It takes resisting the urge to prove your worth by how many hours you stay logged in. It takes honouring your biology instead of overriding it for short-term speed.

Because hustle wears out quickly, but rhythm carries you.

It lets you work with your brain, not against it.

It gives you something hustle can't: longevity, clarity, presence.

This isn't just about doing more with less. It's about living in a way that lets you show up fully, not just once, but again and again.

Not burned out. Not scattered.

Aligned.

# Chapter 20: The Myth of Willpower

We like to think of willpower as a moral trait.

You either have it or you don't. You're either strong or weak. Focused or easily distracted. It's the story we tell ourselves when we can't seem to stay on task, when we reach for the phone again, when we break our promise to do that one crucial thing without interruption. We blame ourselves. We say we need more discipline.

But willpower isn't a character trait. It's a *resource*. And like any resource, it gets depleted.

You can't run all day without rest. You can't stay emotionally available forever without burnout. You can't resist distractions continuously and expect your brain to keep functioning as if nothing's changed. Yet that's precisely what many of us hope when we rely on willpower alone.

It works for a while. At the start of the day, after a good night's sleep, maybe with a strong coffee in hand, you can focus. You can push aside the urge to check your phone, scroll, or bounce between tasks. But by afternoon, something shifts. You lose steam. You break your rules. You tell yourself you'll start again tomorrow.

That's not a weakness. That's depletion.

The prefrontal cortex, the part of your brain responsible for self-control and attention, uses a lot of energy. And just like your muscles fatigue with exertion, so does your capacity to self-regulate. When you rely entirely on willpower to maintain focus, you're asking your brain to run uphill, against the wind, all day long.

Eventually, it gives out. Not because you're lazy. But because the system isn't designed to carry that load forever.

This is why some of the most focused people you know don't necessarily have stronger willpower. They have *better environments*. They've learned to reduce the number of decisions they have to make. They design their space, tools, and schedule to support concentration, rather than constantly resisting temptation.

It's not about having more control. It's about needing less of it.

If your phone is out of reach, you don't need to fight the urge to check it every five minutes. If you've set up a time block for deep work, you don't have to choose between that and ten other competing priorities in real-time. If you've disabled the notifications that fracture your flow, you don't have to pretend you're above their pull.

The goal isn't to become superhuman. It's to become strategic.

Because relying on willpower is like trying to fix a leak by bailing water instead of sealing the hole, you'll stay busy, you'll look productive, but you'll always be on the edge of collapse.

Focus, sustained over time, doesn't come from heroic effort. It comes from creating a context in which attention is the default, not the battle.

That means honouring your limits and recognizing when your energy is low. Taking breaks before your brain begs for them. Saying no to things that fragment you, not because you don't care, but because you do.

It also means knowing that a distracted mind is not always a failing; it's often a message. Something in your environment, your energy, your schedule, isn't supporting what you're trying to do.

Listen to that.

And respond not with shame, but with structure.

Create boundaries that guard your attention.

Design habits that align with your rhythms.

Set up spaces that invite focus instead of fighting for it.

The world will still ask for your willpower. It will test your focus with a thousand little interruptions. But when you stop relying on willpower and start building systems that protect what matters, you'll find something surprising:

Focus begins to feel less like effort and more like home.

# Part III: The Cultural Lie We Call Normal

## Chapter 21: Availability Isn't Accountability

At some point, we stopped asking whether being reachable was the same as being responsible. The shift didn't happen all at once. It began with good intentions, open communication, team collaboration, and fast feedback. Then it hardened into expectation. Now, being available at all times is treated as a default: not a feature, but a requirement.

You see it in the morning email check before breakfast, in the Slack messages answered at red lights, and in the guilt that creeps in after ignoring a group text for an hour. You see it in status indicators and read receipts, in the way people apologize for not replying "sooner," even when their silence lasted mere minutes. The cultural script says: if you're not immediately responsive, you're unreliable.

But that's a lie.

Availability isn't the same as accountability. The former is about constant presence. The latter is about dependable outcomes. One drains your time and energy trying to signal commitment. The other builds trust through quiet, sustained delivery. Yet the two are so often conflated that people begin to shape their entire work identities around reactivity. They respond quickly, attend to everything, and agree to all visibility requests, but then struggle to produce anything of depth. The more connected they are, the less room they have to think.

I remember one client who prided herself on being a hyper-responsive team lead. Her inbox was at zero by 10 a.m. daily, and no message went unread for more than twenty minutes. But her actual priorities, the strategic ones that required real thought, sat untouched for weeks. She was tired, anxious, and constantly "working," but making almost no forward progress on anything that mattered. And still, everyone praised her for being "so on top of things."

This is what happens when speed becomes a proxy for reliability. We reward visibility instead of value. We celebrate fast over focused. But being always reachable doesn't mean you're effective. It just means you're interruptible.

The pressure to always be "on" corrodes focus at a fundamental level. Even when we aren't actively checking messages, the knowledge that we might be pulled away at any moment keeps our attention shallow. It prevents us from descending into deep work, from entering that cognitive state where time blurs and clarity expands. We can't get there if we're half-waiting for a buzz or ding to pull us back out.

What's more insidious is how we internalize this pressure. Eventually, it's not your boss, your colleague, or your friend who demands your availability; it's you. You check out of habit, not instruction. You reply before you even process whether it can wait. You anticipate expectations before they're voiced. You apologize for boundaries you never should've had to defend.

We confuse being "good" with being accessible. And we're burning out in the process.

This dynamic is everywhere. In families, we feel obligated to be instantly responsive to every group chat, even when we're exhausted. In friendships, we worry that silence might be taken personally, that our absence might offend. In the workplace, the notion of "responsiveness" has expanded to cover not just communication but identity. You're not just doing your job; you are performing your availability as part of your worth.

But availability is cheap. It requires no reflection, no prioritization, no self-management. It simply means you're ready to react. Accountability, on the other hand, is expensive. It requires intention, boundaries, and follow-through. It asks you to disappear sometimes, not because you don't care, but because you do. Because you want to show up with something that took time to build.

The real cost of confusing the two is trust erosion, first with others, and then with yourself. You start to doubt your instincts. You hesitate to block time for focused work. You resist saying, "I'll get back to you later," even when you know that's the better path. You stop trusting your deep attention to do what only it can do.

There's no magic solution to this. But there are choices. And it starts with language.

You don't need to apologize for not being instantly available. You need to normalize presence over panic. You need to speak clearly about timelines. "I'll respond tomorrow." "I'm heads-down today, I'll catch up this evening." These aren't evasions. Their structure. And they permit others to protect their time, too.

You also need to reframe how you measure your worth. If your sense of contribution comes from how quickly you respond, you'll never feel caught up, because there will always be more requests. But if your value comes from what you create when no one's watching, you'll start building things that last longer than any thread of messages.

Sometimes the best thing you can offer your team, your client, your family, or yourself is not your constant presence.

It's your undivided one.

And that only exists on the other side of availability.

# Chapter 22: The Open Office Illusion

The first time I worked in an open-plan office, I thought it was my fault that I couldn't concentrate.

Everything looked the way it was supposed to. Sleek desks without partitions, light pouring in through oversized windows, the low buzz of productivity humming in the background. The space was designed to be modern, collaborative, and energizing. But by noon on my first day, I couldn't think.

Not just in a distracted way, but in a disoriented way. I was jumping between email and chat and meetings and side conversations, barely able to track the task I'd set out to do that morning. And yet, no one else seemed to be struggling. They looked busy, like I did, typing, walking, talking, occasionally throwing on headphones, but something about the whole place felt performative, like we were all pretending we were doing deep work when in fact we were making noise.

For a while, I kept the feeling to myself. Maybe I needed to get used to it. Perhaps I wasn't as focused as I thought. Maybe I was the outlier.

Later, I found out I wasn't.

The research is clear, and it's not new. Open-plan offices are one of the most consistent focus-killers in the modern work environment. They were initially conceived as a way to increase communication and reduce hierarchy, breaking down walls and encouraging cross-pollination of ideas. But in practice, they often do the opposite. They increase the number of interruptions and decrease the quality of attention. They don't build collaboration; they erode concentration.

One of the most significant issues is what psychologists call "ambient noise." Unlike focused conversations or relevant sounds, ambient noise creates a low-level cognitive disruption. It's not dramatic, it doesn't startle or distract in an obvious way, but it depletes your ability to maintain mental continuity. The person is coughing at the desk behind you. The lunch chat is two rows over. The sound of someone's keyboard. These aren't emergencies, but your brain can't fully tune them out. It's designed to detect potential threats in your environment, particularly when you don't feel secure due to privacy concerns. So, it scans. It listens. It reacts. And all of that burns your attention in the background, like a dozen tiny programs running silently on your laptop.

There's also the problem of visibility. When you're always seen, even peripheral vision becomes a threat to focus. You become aware of being observed, who's walking past, who's glancing your way, who's standing behind your shoulder. Whether or not anyone is paying attention to you doesn't matter. What matters is that your brain is allocating resources to monitor those possibilities. It's a subtle, sustained pressure. Not enough to feel like surveillance. Just enough to prevent you from going deep.

To compensate, many workers develop rituals. Headphones in, even when no music is playing. An open email draft to look busy. A series of browser tabs is ready to alt-tab in case someone walks by. These are not signs of creative energy; they are signs of cognitive defensiveness. People don't protect their attention because the office supports it. They defend it *despite* the office.

It's not just about sound or movement. It's about the architecture of multitasking. When everything is public, everything becomes potentially interactive. A colleague walking past your desk can interrupt your train of thought with a quick, "Hey, do you have a second?" That second turns into ten minutes, and when you finally get back to your work, the mental thread you were following has unravelled. Multiply that by a few interruptions per day, and your brain begins to anticipate disruption before it happens. You stop thinking fully because you assume you won't be allowed to continue. So, you pre-emptively break your focus. You scatter yourself before the environment can.

Some organizations try to solve this with better tools: noise-cancelling headphones, focus pods, signal flags that say "Do Not Disturb." These help. But they're patches on a deeper issue: we've designed workspaces for frictionless communication, not for deep thinking. We've prioritized access over focus, visibility over clarity.

And it's not just physical layout, it's cultural. When presence is always public, productivity becomes performative. The more open the space, the more visible your effort, and the more tempted you are to make it *look* like you're working instead of doing the hard, invisible, focused work that doesn't photograph well. Thinking deeply doesn't have a sound. Writing a paragraph of real substance might look, from the outside, like staring out a window for fifteen minutes. But in a space that rewards motion over depth, that moment gets interrupted. "Everything okay?" someone might ask. "You look a little stuck."

We've learned to disguise focus as activity. We keep typing so no one questions us. We stay in meetings because presence equals productivity. We over-communicate, respond instantly, and make our inboxes the site of our value. But what we're losing in the process is our ability to think through. To wrestle with a hard idea. To start something and follow it, uninterrupted, to the end.

An open office is not inherently bad. But the way we use it matters. And more often than not, it is a structure that amplifies distraction and normalizes fragmentation.

It doesn't have to be this way.

Some teams are rethinking their defaults: creating quiet zones, setting meeting-free hours, and using asynchronous communication instead of real-time messaging. Others are going hybrid, giving people control over where they do their best work. But the most important shift isn't logistical, it's philosophical.

It's the belief that deep work deserves protection. That your best thinking happens when you're not surrounded by noise. That presence isn't always the most valuable form of contribution.

If we want real focus, we have to stop building environments that assume the mind is available on demand. We need to remember that the best ideas, the best solutions, and the best moments of clarity rarely happen when we're being watched, or when we're half-distracted by everything happening just a few feet away.

They happen in stillness.

They happen in privacy.

They happen when we're allowed to disappear from the noise, long enough to return with something tangible.

84

# Chapter 23: Multitasking Motherhood

There is a phrase we hear often, usually said with admiration, sometimes awe: "She does it all." It's used to describe the woman who works, parents, organizes, manages, plans, maintains, and nurtures, often all in the same hour. The woman who handles dinner while helping with homework, folds laundry while returning calls, runs a meeting with a toddler on her lap, texts back birthday reminders while mentally reviewing tomorrow's schedule. She does it all, we say.

But what we don't say out loud is what it costs her to do it.

Multitasking motherhood isn't just a lifestyle; it's an inheritance. A cultural expectation passed from one generation to the next, shaped by systemic gaps and personal grit, praised for its heroism while quietly exhausting the women who carry its weight.

Unlike other kinds of multitasking, which might happen in sprints, at work, in meetings, during rush hours, this one never stops. It spans time zones and time blocks. It crosses physical and emotional labour. It wraps around weekends, school pick-ups, and midnight wake-ups. It's not a temporary strategy to get through a busy day. It becomes the structure of life itself.

What makes it especially draining isn't just the number of tasks involved, but their diversity. Mothers are not switching between similar items on a checklist. They're toggling between roles with wildly different emotional demands. In twenty minutes, a mother might move from soothing a crying child to reviewing a spreadsheet, from fielding a school email to preparing lunch, from correcting behaviour to responding to a colleague, all while trying to remember the name of the dentist, the time of the recital, and whether she replied to that birthday invitation.

Each of these tasks pulls on a different layer of attention, a different reservoir of energy. The fragmentation doesn't just scatter focus; it dilutes identity. Because multitasking, over time, erodes the boundaries that allow us to feel like whole human beings within any one role. You become so used to dividing your mind that you forget what it feels like to live inside a single moment.

Many mothers will tell you they feel constantly "behind." Not because they're unproductive, but because they're continually interrupted, by others, yes, but also by themselves. There's an internal checklist always running, always alert to the next need. The kitchen counter may be wiped down, but now it's time to prepare a work brief. The groceries may be done, but now there's laundry and a call to return. Even rest gets framed as efficiency. A walk is an opportunity to catch up on messages. A child's nap becomes a chance to squeeze in a meeting.

There is no pause button. There is only the next thing.

What deepens the complexity is that this multitasking is often invisible. Emotional labour, planning, remembering, and anticipating are not things that show up on a spreadsheet. They don't get tracked in time logs. But they are real. They burn cognitive fuel. They tax the nervous system. And when they are unacknowledged, they begin to feel like failures of character rather than the result of carrying too much.

This is why many mothers feel like they're failing, even when they're doing more than most people can see.

And yet, our culture continues to reward this fragmentation. We lift images of women who can handle it all, do it all, and keep smiling through it. We praise the multitasking mom as if her endurance is a sign of strength, instead of evidence of an unsustainable model. We give standing ovations to the mother who manages everything and whisper behind the back of the one who says, "I can't keep doing this."

But saying that isn't a weakness. It's wisdom.

Because the truth is: multitasking motherhood is not sustainable. Not in the long term. Not if what we want is mental health, emotional presence, creative fulfillment, and genuine connection.

The solution isn't found in productivity hacks or better time-blocking. Those tools have value, but they don't solve the deeper problem. The fundamental shift begins with permission, permission for mothers to stop doing it all without apology. Permission to choose presence over performance. Permission to ask for support not as a luxury, but as a right. And permission, above all, to do one thing at a time.

That might mean letting the dishes wait so a conversation with a child can be had without divided attention. It might mean asking a partner to share the mental load, not just the chores. It might mean saying no to one more obligation, even when guilt tries to rise. It might mean creating sacred spaces, an hour, a morning, a weekend, where the mind is allowed to rest in a single focus without interruption.

This isn't selfish. It's self-preservation.

A mind that's constantly split cannot reflect. A heart that's always managing cannot open. A life lived in fragments cannot feel whole. And a mother who never stops multitasking eventually loses touch with the part of herself that longs to be.

That part deserves more than a moment here or there. It deserves room to breathe.

We need to stop celebrating multitasking as the highest form of maternal success. We need to start honouring depth, presence, boundaries, and clarity. These things are not luxuries. They are life-giving.

When a mother is allowed to concentrate, she does not become less available to her family; she becomes more real. More grounded. More human. She is not a machine calibrated to run programs of service. She is a person with her rhythms, her own needs, her longings.

To multitask less is not to love less.

It is to live more fully within each act of love.

And that changes everything.

# Chapter 24: School Is Fragmenting Our Kids

If you want to understand how deeply multitasking has embedded itself into the culture, look at a school schedule.

From the outside, it appears to be structured, with blocks of time, clearly defined subjects, and learning targets printed neatly on the board. Students rotate through various subjects, including math, language arts, science, history, lunch, and electives. The day is divided into pieces, each with a clear beginning and end. But what looks like order is often a blueprint for fragmentation.

The average school day requires students to switch focus every 40 to 60 minutes, often with no transition time, no moment to digest, no space to reflect. The bell rings, and the subject ends. Whether the mind is finished thinking or not doesn't matter. It's time to move on. The next class, the next set of expectations, the following assessment.

This isn't how deep learning happens.

Real learning, the kind that roots itself into long-term memory, that shapes a student's understanding of the world and their place in it, requires time. Not just clock time, but cognitive time. Space to wrestle, to wonder, to follow curiosity through its winding path. And that kind of time is precisely what the structure of most modern schools erodes.

Instead of going deep, students are trained to shift. To switch gears rapidly. To compartmentalize subjects and emotions. To leave a half-formed idea in one room so they can sprint through the hall to a completely unrelated one. Over time, this builds not just fragmented knowledge, but a fragmented way of thinking.

It's a rhythm that teaches kids to prepare for interruption, not flow.

Consider the average morning of a middle schooler: a few minutes of announcements, then a math lesson. Just as they begin to grasp a concept, it's time to pack up. Next is English. They sit, recalibrate, open a book, maybe write a paragraph. The bell rings. Off to science. Then lunch. Then history. Then perhaps an elective or a study hall. Each period begins with catching up and ends with shutting down. Every new classroom brings a shift in expectations, tone, focus, and pace.

That many transitions in a single day might not seem harmful in the short term. But over time, the mental habit it builds is one of shallow presence. You learn to dip into things just enough to complete the task. You skim rather than wrestle. You memorize rather than understand. You manage your time by the clock, not by cognitive readiness.

It's multitasking in disguise.

And when students begin to internalize this rhythm, it doesn't stop at school walls. It follows them home. Homework is often tackled in short bursts, with distractions nearby, such as TV, music, and a phone within reach. Social media pings blend with study sessions. Attention becomes split by default.

But it's not just the schedule that trains this. It's the reward structure.

Students are often praised for output, not insight. For fast responses, not deep ones. For how much they do, not how fully they understand. A child who completes every assignment but doesn't retain the material is often viewed as more successful than the one who thinks deeply, questions the work, and falls behind on speed. And when students are told their value lies in their efficiency, they stop exploring in favour of performing.

What makes this worse is that most children are born with a natural inclination *for depth*. Young kids are naturally immersive. Watch a child build with blocks, or draw, or invent a story with toys; they don't look up. Their attention narrows in the best way. They follow a single line of thought with total presence. And then they enter systems that ask them, bit by bit, to abandon that state in favour of compliance, speed, and multitasking.

We often say we want kids to "pay attention," but we don't provide the structure that would help them maintain it.

We keep them in a constant state of mental pivoting and then wonder why they struggle to focus. We provide them with devices to manage schedules and communication, but we never teach them how to manage their attention. We label some kids as "easily distracted" when, in reality, they are simply reacting to the overstimulated, under-protected environments we've placed them in.

To be clear, none of this is an indictment of teachers. Most educators are doing heroic work inside systems that don't support the very things they know students need. Many want to slow down. They want more time for discussion, more room for questions, and more trust in curiosity. But they're bound by policies, testing standards, rigid timelines, and overcrowded classrooms. They are navigating the same culture of fragmentation as their students, often with less time, less support, and more pressure.

The larger issue isn't individual, it's systemic.

And unless we confront the way multitasking is built into the architecture of how we educate, we'll keep training kids not to think deeply, but to shift quickly. We'll prepare them for a world of notifications and tabs and shallow scrolling, and in doing so, we'll rob them of the deeper capacities they were born to develop: reflection, wonder, focus.

This doesn't mean we need to overhaul the entire system overnight. But it does mean we need to start asking more complex questions. What would it look like to protect attention in the classroom? What if students had fewer transitions, more project-based learning, and longer blocks of time to work deeply? What if we taught not just content, but cognitive rhythm? What if we honored depth the same way we currently honor productivity?

The future will not belong to the children who can juggle the most tasks at once.

It will belong to those who can think through complexity without running from it. To those who can sit with uncertainty, follow one idea down, and emerge not with a quick answer, but with fundamental understanding.

And that kind of thinking starts not with more apps, more content, or more noise.

It starts with space.

With slowness.

With the radical idea that one deep thought is worth more than ten shallow ones.

That's how we begin to unfragment the next generation.

# Chapter 25: Meetings Are Killing Your Brain

There's a strange phenomenon in modern work culture: the more meetings we have, the less it feels like anything is getting done.

You log on in the morning, maybe with a list in mind, a plan to tackle one or two deep-focus items that matter. But before you even reach for that first real task, your calendar reminds you: you're already late—a daily check-in, a project sync, a team alignment call, a cross-functional update. You sit in each one, nodding, occasionally contributing, sometimes zoning out, until suddenly it's 3 p.m. and your real work hasn't even started.

For a long time, we treated this as usual. Meetings were synonymous with collaboration. To meet was to work. To be invited was to matter. To decline was to risk invisibility. So we said yes. Again and again. We booked our calendars into gridlock. We overcommitted ourselves and called it team spirit.

But here's the thing most people won't say aloud: meetings are not neutral. They don't just "take time", they take attention. And in the process, they take energy, depth, and cognitive space that we never fully get back during the day.

Your brain, whether you realize it or not, is paying a toll for every meeting it attends.

The cost starts before the meeting even begins. Knowing you have a meeting in thirty minutes changes how you work. You may not start a challenging task because you know you'll be interrupted. You may skim instead of concentrate, scan instead of sink in. That's one of the quiet damages of constant meetings; they fracture the day into fragments too small for real thinking.

Then there's the switch cost. Every time you move from deep work into a meeting, or from a meeting back to a solo task, your brain has to shift contexts. This isn't instant. Studies show it can take more than twenty minutes for the brain to re-enter a state of deep focus after an interruption, especially one as cognitively demanding as a meeting. That means even a quick 30-minute sync can consume over an hour of functional productivity, not just the block on your calendar.

And while some meetings are necessary, many are not. We hold meetings out of habit, out of fear, or due to a cultural assumption that discussing the work is equivalent to doing it. But often, the meetings themselves become the work. We share status updates instead of creating solutions. We report progress rather than make progress. We clarify intentions without clarifying outcomes.

Even worse, many meetings are performative. People show up to be seen, to avoid being left out, to prove they're "engaged." They speak in vague summaries, nod through redundant slide decks, and take notes on things they already knew. No one wants to be the one who says, "This could've been an email." So we continue, politely wasting one another's best hours.

There's also the group dynamic to consider. Meetings introduce subtle social pressures. You monitor how you're perceived. You track tone, body language, and hierarchy. You may hold back ideas because the room doesn't feel safe, or overstate things. After all, silence feels awkward. Your brain burns energy on navigating relationships, not solving problems. In some cases, that's necessary. But in most cases, it's not a wise use of mental energy.

Now imagine this rhythm, every day, for years. What does that do to our ability to think deeply? To generate original ideas? To engage with complexity instead of merely reporting around it?

The real tragedy is that many of the people most affected by meeting overload are the same people we count on to do the most valuable cognitive work: designers, developers, analysts, strategists, educators, and creatives. People whose most significant contributions come not in meetings, but in sustained, uninterrupted time to focus and make.

We often hear about "collaboration fatigue," but that's a polite phrase for something more serious: attention erosion. When your day is sliced into a dozen conversations, when your brain is asked to jump tracks every hour, when your ability to enter flow is cut short by calendar alerts, you are not just losing time; you are losing the ability to go deep at all.

Some companies try to address this by introducing "No Meeting Wednesdays" or scheduling focus hours. These are a start. But the solution isn't just in rearranging the calendar. It's in shifting the assumption that meetings are the default mode of collaboration.

Meetings should be the exception, not the rule. They should be held only when there's a clear problem to solve, a decision to make, or a conversation that requires real-time human nuance. They should have fewer people in the room. They should have a defined start, a sharp focus, and a definitive end. And they should *never* be used as a substitute for trust, clarity, or leadership.

If your team can't operate without constant meetings, that's not a sign of engagement; it's a sign of dysfunction.

The alternative is not isolation. It's intentionality.

It's reclaiming time not just for the sake of less, but for the sake of better. Better thinking. Better contributions. Better relationships are based on the trust that when people are allowed to focus, they will do the work that matters.

You don't need to be in every meeting to be a valuable teammate.

You don't need to "check in" constantly to lead.

You don't need to speak up on Zoom to prove your worth.

You need space.

You need continuity.

You need time to follow your thoughts through to their conclusion.

Because real collaboration doesn't happen in endless meetings.

It happens when people are given the time to do their best work, so they have something meaningful to bring back to the table when it counts.

# Chapter 26: The Rise of Shallow Work

The workday is full.

That's the feeling most people carry. Full inbox. Full calendar. Full task list. From the moment your eyes open, your mind is already in motion, checking notifications, scanning your schedule, queuing the day's demands in your head before your feet hit the floor. You stay busy from morning until night. There are messages to answer, threads to follow, and requests to acknowledge. You log off late, not because you were idle, but because there was too much to do.

And yet, at the end of all that effort, a quiet truth nags at you: you didn't do anything *deep*.

You were working, yes. But not the kind that moves the needle. Not the kind that demands full attention and produces lasting value. Instead, your day was spent in what Cal Newport famously called *shallow work*: tasks that are logistical, reactive, repetitive, or easy to replicate. And in our current culture, these tasks don't just exist. They dominate.

Shallow work looks like productivity. It feels like effort. But it rarely creates something original or meaningful. It keeps the engine running without moving the car. You spend hours answering emails, updating decks, filling in reports, joining check-ins, and adjusting small details, but the deeper thinking that makes those details matter never quite happens.

The conditions for this shift didn't arrive overnight. They crept in, slowly, through good intentions and poor design. First came the tools: email, then instant messaging, task managers, collaboration platforms, shared docs, and project dashboards.

Each one promised more efficiency, better coordination, seamless teamwork. But what they delivered, in practice, was an always-on flood of micro-demands.

The problem isn't the tools themselves, it's how we use them. Most knowledge workers now spend more time *discussing their work* than actually doing it. They spend hours planning, aligning, syncing, and checking in. By the time the real work window opens, if it opens at all, the mind is scattered and fatigued.

The deeper problem is that these tools shape not just what we do, but how we think. They train the brain to expect interruption. They normalize task-switching. They reward responsiveness over reflection. Before long, your day becomes an endless loop of triage, deciding what to click on, what to answer, what to avoid, and what to defer.

That's the hallmark of shallow work: your attention is pulled, not chosen.

And because shallow work is easier to quantify, it's easier to reward. Managers can see who responded quickly. They can measure the number of tasks completed, the number of emails sent, and the number of tickets closed. But what they often can't see is the quality of thought—the hidden work. The hours spent wrestling with a complex idea, quietly, offscreen. The kind of focus that produces a strategy, a breakthrough, a piece of writing that resonates.

So what gets measured is what gets done.

And what gets done is what's easy to display.

The result is a culture where depth is pushed to the margins. It gets squeezed between meetings, wedged into commutes, or postponed until after hours. You do your "real" work at night, not because you prefer it, but because it's the only time no one is pinging you. You think best on weekends, not because you're a workaholic, but because it's the only time your brain has room to stretch.

This isn't sustainable. It's cognitive debt. And just like financial debt, it accrues interest.

Shallow work doesn't just waste time; it weakens our intellectual muscles. When you spend all day reacting, you lose the habit of thinking proactively. You start forgetting how to follow an idea beyond a single paragraph. You skim more, pause less. You seek speed, not insight.

That degradation isn't just personal. It shows up in the quality of everything: our writing becomes more generic, our decisions more rushed, our relationships more transactional. We talk more than we mean to. We produce more than we believe in. We show up to the project, but we leave our minds behind.

But it doesn't have to stay this way.

The first step is not to ban shallow work. It has its place. Logistics still matter. Communication is necessary. Support tasks keep systems functioning. The goal is not to eliminate shallow work; it's to *contain* it. To prevent it from devouring the hours meant for focus.

That means being ruthless about boundaries. It means scheduling fundamental blocks of deep work, uninterrupted, protected, offline if needed, and defending those blocks as if they were meetings with your highest self. It means turning off notifications, closing email tabs, setting status to "unavailable," and meaning it.

It also means redesigning collaboration. Teams should be encouraged to solve problems asynchronously whenever possible. A two-hour meeting can often be replaced with a shared doc and twenty minutes of real writing. A status update doesn't always require a call; it can be a thoughtful message, written with care and read without pressure. This is not less human, it's more respectful. It gives people space to think before they speak. To listen without rushing to respond.

And above all, it means redefining what we value. A single insight drawn from deep focus is worth more than twenty status reports. One well-crafted proposal can outperform a week of reactive emails. The ability to think clearly, create deeply, and decide wisely is not just a soft skill. It's the foundation of every hard result we care about.

If we want better work, more creative, more meaningful, more effective, we have to stop idolizing the busy blur of shallow productivity.

Because the most critical work you will do will never come from your inbox.

It will come from that quiet place just beyond distraction, where your full attention finally has room to land, and stay.

# Chapter 27: Toxic Productivity

There is a kind of exhaustion that doesn't come from working hard; it comes from working *constantly*.

Not from lifting heavy things or running long miles, but from carrying a never-ending sense that you should be doing more. More checking. More updating. More achieving. More proving. Even when you're resting, even when you're technically off, the mental engine never shuts down. You feel behind before the day starts. You measure your worth in output. You can't remember the last time you finished something and truly felt done.

This is toxic productivity.

At first glance, it looks like ambition. From the outside, you might appear high performing, disciplined, and dependable. People compliment your drive. You say yes, stay late, show up early. You check off the list, then make a new one. It feels suitable for a while until that good feeling becomes dependent on the following item, task, or surge of validation.

Then it doesn't feel like driving anymore. It feels like a compulsion.

Toxic productivity is different from hard work. It's not about effort, it's about *identity*. It's when doing becomes the only thing that makes you feel worthy. When rest feels like guilt. When pausing feels like failure, when you can't stop because if you stop, you're afraid of what that might say about you.

It's not a new problem, but technology has made it easier to hide and harder to escape. You can always do "just one more thing." Respond to one more email. Edit one more file. Organize one more list. Even leisure starts to feel like something to optimize. Meditation becomes a productivity tool. Exercise becomes a metric. Even sleep is tracked, measured, and gamified.

Eventually, everything becomes work in disguise.

You don't just read, you read to learn something applicable. You don't just go for a walk; you listen to a podcast to stay informed. You don't just have a conversation, you network. Every activity must produce something. Every moment must be squeezed for value. Even joy becomes functional.

This mindset is reinforced everywhere. You hear it in advice like "grind now, rest later," or "if you're not working on your dream, someone else is." Hustle culture wraps fear in aspiration. It tells you that to slow down is to fall behind. That someone, somewhere, is outworking you. That is, unless you keep producing, you are wasting your potential.

But this is a lie built on a dangerous assumption: that human beings are machines. That we can run at full capacity, without breaks, forever.

We can't.

Burnout is not just a side effect of toxic productivity; it is its inevitable conclusion. And not just physical burnout, but emotional and cognitive depletion. You lose the ability to think clearly. You become reactive, unfocused, and irritable. Small tasks feel overwhelming. Decisions become harder. You might still look productive on the outside, but inside, you're running on fumes.

And the deeper cost is invisible: you lose your sense of self outside of what you produce. You don't know how to sit still anymore. You don't know how to enjoy something without turning it into a project. You don't know how to measure your day without a scoreboard. You become terrified of what silence might reveal.

The antidote to toxic productivity isn't laziness, it's meaning.

It's remembering why you're working in the first place. What you're working *for*. What success looks like when you take away the metrics, the dashboards, the applause. It's asking whether your effort is building something you care about, or whether it's just keeping you busy enough to avoid the more profound questions.

To heal from this kind of productivity sickness, you don't need to quit everything. You need to start drawing lines.

You start by asking: What's *enough*?

What's enough for today? Enough for this week? Enough to be proud of without spiralling into shame? Most people have no concept of enough. They only know more. So they keep pushing, chasing, escalating the target. But enough is the only way to reclaim peace.

Then you ask: What is this effort serving?

Are you moving toward something meaningful, or are you trying to escape a feeling? Are you creating from purpose, or reacting from fear? Are you building a life, or just padding a résumé?

And finally, you ask: what would it look like to stop, not permanently, but just for now?

Close the laptop and avoid opening another tab. To take a walk without checking anything. To sit without a plan. To let the moment be complete in itself, without requiring it to generate value.

You won't get applause for this. You won't be rewarded for rest in most work cultures. But that's why it's radical, because it refuses the myth that worth is earned through exhaustion. Because it honours the parts of you that exist outside of productivity. Because it declares, quietly and clearly, that you are already enough.

And in that space, in that stillness, you may find that the best ideas, the most profound clarity, the most real connections, none of them came when you were grinding.

They came when you finally stopped.

# Chapter 28: Digital Servitude

The promise of technology was freedom.

Freedom from drudgery, from repetition, from inefficiency. The tools were designed to handle mundane tasks, automate processes, store information, and connect us instantly across time zones. They were supposed to save us time.

But something strange happened. Instead of working less, we began working more. Instead of freeing our minds, we've filled them with more tabs, feeds, alerts, dashboards, and requests. Instead of using the tools, the tools started using us.

What began as a relationship of utility became one of servitude.

It's not that we don't benefit from digital tools. Of course, we do. A well-designed platform can streamline collaboration. A note-taking app can preserve ideas we'd otherwise lose. A calendar can organize a chaotic day. But these tools were meant to serve human attention, not hijack it.

And increasingly, that's what they do.

The apps we use daily are not neutral. Most are designed, at least in part, to capture and hold your focus, not to support it. Notifications, badges, animations, red dots, infinite scroll- these aren't features by accident. They're part of an attention economy built on engagement metrics. They train you to check more often, stay longer, and respond faster. Your attention becomes currency.

You think you're managing your inbox. But really, your inbox is managing you.

You think you're controlling your tools. But look closely: how many of your actions each day are reactions? How often are you pulled into an app you didn't intend to open, responding to a message you didn't plan to see, clicking something you didn't ask for?

This is the essence of digital servitude: you're not acting from intention; you're acting from trigger.

The average knowledge worker now switches tasks every three minutes, often prompted by an external alert or internal itch to check. That's not because we're undisciplined. It's because the tools are designed to reward interruption. There is always something new to look at. Always someone is waiting. Always a platform inviting you to keep scrolling, clicking, and refreshing.

Over time, this rewires your brain. It lowers your tolerance for stillness. It makes silence feel empty. It creates a kind of background anxiety that pushes you to fill every gap with more input.

And then there's the problem of *tools stacking on top of tools*. We use Slack to replace email, then check both. We use Asana to manage projects, but still create spreadsheets to track the work. We sync calendars, apps, threads, files, and still spend half the day figuring out where the real work lives. The system becomes more complex, not less.

You end up managing the tools instead of letting the tools manage the work.

This isn't just inefficient, it's cognitively expensive. Every platform has its interface, logic, and way of formatting tasks and structuring conversations. Every switch between systems incurs a small cost. Multiply that by dozens of interactions a day, and you're burning energy just navigating the layers—no wonder we're tired before we've done anything meaningful.

But the most dangerous part of digital servitude isn't time, it's *identity drift*. When your entire day is spent responding to tools, you stop asking what matters. You become someone who checks, clears, updates, and syncs. You become efficient at managing noise. But you forgot how to listen for the signal.

And then, gradually, you forget what deep focus even feels like.

You try to write something important, but your mind keeps drifting. You try to sit still, but your fingers reach for your phone. You try to think through a problem, but your brain wants a quick hit of novelty. That's not because you lack discipline. It's because your environment has trained you to be interruptible.

You didn't choose this, not fully. But you do have a choice now.

You can choose to reclaim attention. To invert the relationship. To make the tools serve *you* again.

That starts with friction. You introduce barriers between your mind and the noise. You turn off notifications. You remove apps from your home screen. You set specific times to check messages, rather than treating every moment as an open window.

It also means designing your digital life like you'd design a physical workspace. What do you *need* on your desk? What creates clarity instead of clutter? What apps help you focus, and which ones increase the sense of urgency without absolute necessity?

Most of all, it means remembering that you are not an interface. You are not a tab manager. You are not a notification center. You are a human being with deep cognitive powers that require care, intention, and protection.

The best parts of your brain, the insight, the synthesis, the vision, don't show up when you're chasing pings.

They show up in silence. n slowness. In single-tasking. Technology should amplify those states, not override them. If it doesn't, you have permission to opt out. To close the tab. To uninstall the app. To reclaim the mental space that was never meant to be outsourced to a blinking screen.

This is not nostalgia for a simpler time. It is a call to responsibility because every minute you give to a tool that doesn't respect your attention is a minute you take from something that might have mattered more.

And in the end, your tools should work *for* you.

Not the other way around.

# Chapter 29: Why Companies Don't Value Depth

In many organizations, the people doing the most critical thinking are often the least visible.

They're not in every meeting. They don't respond to emails within minutes. They may be quiet in group chats, slow to speak up on Zoom, and hard to schedule time with. But when they *do* show up and deliver, they bring something no one else has. An insight. A solution. A sentence so clear it realigns the entire conversation.

And yet, in the modern workplace, these people often go unrecognized. Not because they lack value, but because they don't match the performance of productivity that many companies mistake for excellence.

This is one of the great paradoxes of the modern work culture: we say we value depth, but we reward speed. We claim to want focus, yet we promote accessibility. We talk about thought leadership, but our systems tend to elevate the most reactive individuals —the ones who are always available, constantly updating, and always present in the visible arenas.

This culture didn't appear by accident. It's a product of measurement. Once technology gave us dashboards and data, we started trying to quantify everything. How many hours worked? How many emails were sent? How many tickets were closed? How many projects were "touched"? But what we couldn't measure, what doesn't fit cleanly into a spreadsheet, is deep thought.

There's no metric for wrestling with an idea for four hours and emerging with one perfect paragraph. There's no KPI for resisting distractions long enough to build something cohesive. No performance tracker rewards are *not responding* to every request, so you can finish what matters.

And so, in the absence of metrics for depth, companies reward what they can see: activity. Availability. Volume.

A manager might say they trust their team to focus, but if you don't answer your Slack message within a few minutes, questions start to bubble. Are you away from your desk? Are you unengaged? Are you working on the wrong thing? Never mind that you were deep into writing, designing, building, and solving. What matters is the surface signal—the performance of effort.

And what gets rewarded gets repeated.

So, people adapt. They reply quickly, even if distracted. They say yes to meetings they don't need. They over-communicate, over-report, and over-explain. They make themselves visible, not because it's valuable, but because invisibility feels risky.

You can't blame them. In a system that values attention over intention, the safest thing to do is to be constantly reachable.

But over time, this creates a culture where deep work becomes a liability. Where the people who *protect* their time are viewed as "difficult," "slow," or "not a team player." Where deep thinkers are asked to do shallow tasks, to signal participation, where the noise gets louder, and the signal gets lost.

Some leaders see the problem. They say things like, "We want fewer meetings," or "We support focus time." But unless the incentives change, nothing else will because culture doesn't live in slogans. It lives in behaviour. It lives in what gets praised, what gets promoted, what gets modelled from the top down.

If a senior leader sends messages at midnight, people learn that responsiveness matters more than rest. If the most visible employee gets the most praise, people learn to prioritize appearance over output. If the person who takes time to think gets passed over for the person who reacts quickly, the message is clear: thinking is a risk.

And yet, here's the irony: most companies *need* deep work more than ever.

The easy problems have already been automated. The low-hanging fruit is gone. What's left are the complex problems, the ones that require insight, creativity, and sustained attention. Strategic decisions. New ideas. Thoughtful communication. Coherent product design. These are not shallow tasks. They require time. They require space. They require people who can say, "I need the afternoon to think," and not be penalized for it.

But you can't unlock that thinking with back-to-back calls and nonstop messaging. You can't create clarity when your team is constantly asked to react. You can't build something meaningful in a culture that only rewards the metrics of movement.

So how do we shift it?

First, by naming the gap. Companies must explicitly acknowledge that there is a difference between busyness and value. That a quiet day on Slack may mean someone is in the zone, not that they're slacking off. That deep work often looks like nothing on the outside, but is doing everything that matters on the inside.

Second, by creating incentives for depth. Don't just say focus matters; measure it: track outcomes, not just activity. Ask teams to report not just what they *did*, but what they *finished*. Make room in schedules for uninterrupted time. Celebrate thoughtful ideas, not just fast ones.

Third, by modelling from leadership. If you're a manager or executive, your behaviour sets the tone. Protect your focus, and talk about why. Don't send midnight messages unless you genuinely want to normalize midnight work. Don't require instant replies. Show your team that depth is allowed. That thinking slowly isn't the same as moving slowly.

And finally, by reframing value. Remind your team regularly that it's not the person who juggles the most who wins. It's the person who finishes what matters. Who creates with care. Who contributes something real.

Because in the long run, depth is not a luxury. It's a necessity.

And if companies don't start valuing it now, they will lose the very people capable of delivering it.

# Chapter 30: Culture Isn't a To-Do List

Every company claims to want a strong culture.

It's plastered on websites, embedded in mission statements, threaded into onboarding slides. Culture is framed as the invisible glue that binds teams, the magic that makes great things happen. Leaders say it's the priority behind every policy. Executives post about it. Departments create initiatives around it. Culture becomes a project, a brand, a promise.

And then, somewhere along the way, it becomes a checklist.

Run a wellness program. Offer snacks. Create a values document. Plan quarterly off-sites. Host a few training sessions on communication or mindfulness. Maybe roll out a feedback tool or a team-building game. And when all that's done, declare: "We care about culture."

But culture doesn't live in lists.

It lives in lived experience.

And the truth, quiet and uncomfortable, is that many of the companies that talk the most about culture are still built on the patterns that fragment it: overwork, constant availability, shallow communication, and performative productivity. Their calendars are still packed. Their people are still burnt out. Their attention is still scattered. And no number of pizza Fridays or branded mugs can fix that.

Because culture isn't what you *say* it is.

Culture is what you *allow*.

It's who gets praised and who gets ignored. It's what behaviours are tolerated. It's how decisions are made when no one is looking. It's how people feel when they're under pressure.

It's what happens when someone says, "I need time to think", and whether that's respected or penalized.

And for too many companies, despite all the culture talk, the real message is clear: move fast. Be visible. Stay reachable. Look busy.

People learn quickly that attention isn't protected. That taking time for deep work isn't safe. That whoever reacts fastest gets rewarded. That meetings matter more than outcomes. That saying no, even to protect quality, can make you seem disengaged. That thinking isn't valued unless it's done out loud, in real time, on a call.

And so, even in cultures that claim to value creativity, connection, and wellbeing, people adapt. They multitask through meetings. They check messages at dinner. They reply to emails with half a brain. They finish their "real work" at night. They stop asking big questions because they never have time to hear the answers.

They burn out and blame themselves.

They assume they just aren't disciplined enough. If they were more organized, they could juggle better. That if they time-blocked harder, the overwhelm would go away. They internalize the noise as failure. And the company, watching them move fast and stay busy, assumes culture is working.

But motion isn't engagement.

And visibility isn't a contribution.

Authentic culture is something slower, quieter, and more challenging to measure. It's a thousand tiny choices made in alignment with what matters. It's the safety to pause. The space to think. The expectation that people are not machines. The belief that depth is worth waiting for.

That kind of culture doesn't emerge from slogans. It grows from structure. It requires systems that match the values on the wall. It requires leadership that models what it claims to care about. It requires patience. Clarity. Courage.

It requires letting go of the illusion that multitasking is a virtue.

And it requires something else, too, something uncomfortable: It requires not being liked all the time.

Because in an authentic culture of focus, some things will have to go. Some meetings will be cancelled. Some deadlines will be extended. Some instant replies will become slower, more thoughtful ones. Some "urgent" things will be challenged. The pace may shift. The noise may drop.

And when it does, some people will feel uncomfortable. They'll miss the adrenaline of the buzz. They'll feel a little exposed, unsure what to do with the new space. They'll have to reckon with how much of their identity was wrapped up in the performance of productivity.

But others, the ones you most need to retain, will exhale.

They'll begin to do their best work again. Not because they were lazy before, but because now, finally, the structure allows it. They'll think through problems instead of rushing to patch them. They'll write clearly. Build carefully. Lead without panic. Listen fully.

And they'll stay, not because of the perks, or the statements, or the swag, but because the culture gave them something rare: dignity.

The dignity to concentrate. To follow their mind instead of fighting it. To finish what they started. To be seen not as a machine, but as a mind. That is what authentic culture does.

And you won't find it on a checklist.

# Part IV: Rebuilding Your Brain's Focus

## Chapter 31: Subtraction, Not Addition

It's easy to believe that if you're struggling to focus, you need a better system.

That's what the internet promises, after all. Search for productivity help, and you'll find thousands of tools, each claiming to be the solution. Apps that block distractions. Extensions that track your time. Templates, frameworks, colour-coded calendars, AI-assisted workflows. There's a solution for every pain point, a tool for every challenge.

So we download, subscribe, and install. We build dashboards and customize routines. We believe that if we can get it all to click, the right combination of software and self-discipline, we'll finally become the focused, efficient person we imagine ourselves to be.

But after the initial rush of setup fades, most of us find that not much has changed. The noise is still there. The pull to check is still there. The struggle to sustain attention remains.

Because the problem isn't that we lack tools, it's that we've confused focus with control.

Proper focus doesn't come from adding more layers to manage your time. It comes from removing the things that don't deserve it.

It starts with subtraction.

This isn't glamorous. It doesn't look like optimization. It seems like turning things off and logging out. Uninstalling. Letting go of systems that are clever but unnecessary. Saying no to digital clutter in the same way you might declutter a room, not because the objects are bad, but because they take up space you can no longer afford to rent out.

You can't recover deep focus if your attention is constantly splintered by things you didn't choose. And most of us, if we're honest, didn't choose most of the noise. We just accumulated it.

We signed up for newsletters we don't read. We installed apps we never questioned. We joined platforms because everyone else did. We let notifications pile up like static. Then we blamed ourselves for being distracted, instead of asking whether our environment was unlivable.

Subtraction is the first real step back toward presence.

And it requires a different kind of intelligence, not the intelligence of systems-building, but of discernment. The ability to ask, again and again, "What is this taking from me?"

Take your phone, for example. Most people use dozens of apps but *intentionally* open only a few. The rest pull them in out of habit. Not because the app adds value, but because it exists. It's there. A tap away. And over time, these low-grade interruptions become part of the architecture of your day. You scroll without deciding to scroll. You check without needing to check. You react, again and again, without ever feeling like you *chose* to.

You can't out-discipline this kind of design. You can't time-manage your way past it. You have to *remove it*.

The solution isn't to create a tighter schedule that includes all these distractions in their little containers. It's to eliminate what doesn't belong. To look at every tool, every account, every habit, and ask: If I hadn't already committed to this, would I add it now?

That's the subtraction mindset.

It doesn't mean cutting everything. But it does mean starting from zero and defaulting to less, and then deciding what gets your attention *on purpose*, rather than by momentum.

Most people overestimate what they need to function and underestimate how much their systems cost them in cognitive residue. They believe focus is a result of better management, but in reality, it's usually a result of less management altogether.

You need fewer tabs. Fewer dashboards. Fewer input streams.

More often than not, the tools designed to help you work end up becoming your work.

You spend twenty minutes setting up a task list, only to realize you haven't started the task. You fiddle with your calendar, adjusting time blocks you don't adhere to. You reply to comments on a platform that wasn't necessary in the first place. You're not lazy, you're caught in a recursive loop where managing focus replaces *having* it.

So you begin, instead, with quiet. You start with subtraction. You uninstall the apps you no longer use. You mute notifications that don't add value. You unfollow accounts that leave your brain feeling scattered. You unsubscribe.

You log out.

You create gaps, not to fill them later, but to leave them empty. Because emptiness is not a lack of value, it is the condition in which focus becomes possible again.

This won't be comfortable. In the beginning, it feels like something is missing. The impulse to check will spike. The mind will search for stimulation. You'll wonder what you're not seeing, what you're not doing, who might be trying to reach you. But if you stay with it, something begins to shift.

You begin to feel time again.

Not the frantic, fragmented time of multitasking, but real time. Expansive, uninterrupted, alive. The kind of time that doesn't demand anything from you. The kind that invites you to notice your thoughts. To trace one of them, slowly, without jumping. To stay.

That is what subtraction gives you.

Not emptiness.

Presence.

# Chapter 32: The First Hour Rule

What you do with your first hour tells your brain what kind of day it's going to be.

Before your calendar fills, before the emails start landing, before Slack lights up and texts begin their silent demands, there's a window. Small, often fragile. It's the moment between waking and reacting, the space where your attention is most awake, even if your body isn't. And it's there, in that first hour, that the tone of your thinking is set.

Most people give it away.

They wake to an alarm that's also a phone, and that phone is also a portal. One swipe, and they're gone, absorbed in notifications, messages, updates, news, nonsense. The eyes are barely open, but already the mind is filling, scrolling, sorting, reacting. And what could've been a clean start becomes a rush of borrowed urgency.

By the time they sit down to work, assuming they haven't already opened their laptop in bed, their brain is already splintered. Not because the day got hard, but because they invited the noise in before they even had a chance to choose.

That's what the First Hour Rule tries to protect.

The idea is simple, though not always easy: for the first sixty minutes of your day, don't give your attention away. Not to email. Not to social feeds. Not to chat apps. Not even to a dozen small, benign to-dos. Protect that first hour like sacred ground. Because in cognitive terms, it is.

Your mental state in the first hour carries more weight than most people realize. It's when your brain is closest to its natural rhythm, unburdened (briefly) by the accumulation of input. You're still emerging from the residue of sleep. If you don't interrupt it with the world's noise, there's a softness there, space to think clearly, to feel out what matters, to begin your day as the author of your attention rather than the recipient of everyone else's.

This isn't about perfection. There are mornings when kids are crying, alarms fail, and the real world makes quiet impossible. But it's not about calm in the external sense; it's about direction. It's about choosing to start the day by *listening inward*, instead of reacting outward.

There are many ways to apply the First Hour Rule. For some, it means diving directly into deep creative work, writing, coding, designing, while the mind is still fresh. For others, it might mean thinking without distraction: journaling, reading, walking without headphones, making coffee without opening a screen. For some, it's planning: looking at your day and deciding *on purpose*, what matters before the flood begins.

What it doesn't mean is multitasking.

It doesn't mean catching up on emails while you eat, or skimming news while dressing, or replying to Slack messages from your phone under the table. That's the point: you're not dividing this hour, you're devoting it.

And it matters more than you think. Because the brain is trained by rhythm and repetition. The way you start one day becomes easier to repeat the next. The first hour becomes a groove in your attention, a track you can follow. If you always begin in reactivity, your whole day will echo that rhythm. If you start in person, it echoes that instead.

There's research behind this. Studies in behavioural psychology show that habits formed in the morning are more likely to persist. There's less cognitive resistance, less decision fatigue. What you practice in that early window becomes part of your mental infrastructure. Which means that hour isn't just a bonus, it's a leverage point.

You don't need to be a morning person. You don't need to meditate at sunrise or journal in a leather-bound notebook. This isn't about aesthetics. It's about *ownership*. It's about reclaiming the one part of the day that is most often sacrificed to noise.

And yes, it requires intention.

Most people resist this at first because their phones are their comfort zone. They want to know what happened overnight. They want to check in, just quickly. But that quick check becomes twenty minutes. That swipe becomes a vortex. That "just one message" becomes the day's first decision, and it was someone else's.

Breaking that cycle requires a few key elements. It takes a plan. Know, the night before, what you're going to do in that first hour. Please don't leave it to impulse. Set it aside, literally, in your calendar. Create friction between you and the distractions by turning off Wi-Fi, using airplane mode, and charging your phone outside the bedroom. Make the cost of reaction slightly higher, and the path to intention marginally easier.

Then, when the morning comes, do *only one thing*. Let it be slow. Let it be single-tasked. Let it be yours.

And watch what happens. Watch how much clearer you are by 9 a.m. Watch how fewer things feel urgent. Watch how the rest of the day stops owning you. Because that first hour? It's not just about productivity.

It's about dignity.

It's a way of saying: my attention belongs to me.

# Chapter 33: Creating a Deep Work Ritual

Focus doesn't happen by accident.

It's not a matter of willpower alone. It doesn't appear the moment you want it to. You don't sit down at a desk, open your laptop, and suddenly fall into flow. That's the myth we carry, that good work is just a matter of trying harder. That if we care enough, we'll concentrate.

But deep focus isn't summoned. It's invited.

And like anything meaningful, it responds to rhythm.

This is where ritual enters.

Not routine, not just a series of steps you repeat out of obligation. Ritual is different. It has intention. It has a shape. It signals something to your brain: *we are entering a different mode now*. It creates a boundary between the ordinary and the focused, between the reactive and the deliberate.

Most people skip this part. They rush from task to task, call to call, errand to inbox, without any real transition. They expect their minds to switch gears instantly. But the brain doesn't work that way. It needs a ramp. A cue. A signal that it's safe and necessary to go deep.

A ritual doesn't need to be elaborate. It just needs to be consistent.

It might start with something as simple as closing every browser tab except one, or lighting a candle and putting on noise-cancelling headphones, and pouring coffee in the same mug every morning, and sitting in the same chair. It could be a walk around the block. A song you always start with—the act of handwriting your intention for the next two hours on a sticky note.

Whatever it is, it needs to be repeatable and purposeful. Something that becomes associated, physically, emotionally, neurologically, with deep work.

Because the real power of ritual isn't just in preparing your tools, it's in preparing *yourself*.

It's in telling your nervous system: now, we're not scanning anymore. We're not checking. We're not responding. We're entering.

This works because the brain loves patterns. Once it associates specific cues with a particular mode of thinking, the transition becomes faster and smoother. You don't have to "feel ready" every time. The ritual itself makes you ready.

And over time, it becomes automatic.

Your body knows: this mug, this space, this light, this sound, this is where focus lives. You feel it settle. You think the outside shrink. You stop glancing around. The mind begins to stay.

For many people, that experience is unfamiliar. Most modern work trains the opposite. It trains scatteredness. Quick replies. Fast shifts. Low-stakes engagement. So when you first start creating a deep work ritual, it may feel awkward. You may resist it, rush it, or doubt its value.

But trust this: the brain responds to repetition.

Keep showing up to the same threshold, and eventually, the door will open faster.

That's why it's essential to protect the ritual itself.

Don't dilute it by doing shallow tasks during that time. Don't blur the line by slipping in email or messages. Don't multitask. Ritual depends on clarity. If you mix your deep work time with everything else, your brain will stop trusting the signal.

The goal isn't perfection. You won't hit flow every time. But what you *will* build is something more important: stability—the mental equivalent of a well-worn trail through a dense forest. You don't have to bushwhack your way through every morning. The path is there. You've walked it before.

And that reliability, that invitation to drop in, is what most people are missing.

They're not lacking ideas. They're lacking structure. Not inspiration, but containment.

Ritual offers that.

It gives focus a home.

And there's something sacred about that, even in the most secular settings. To light a candle and open a notebook. To silence a phone and begin. To say, in your quiet way, this matters enough to protect.

Because deep work is not casual, it's not rushed. It's not something you squeeze between meetings.

It's a state of being.

And it deserves a doorway.

# Chapter 34: Boundaries Are the New Discipline

For most of your life, you were probably taught that discipline meant pushing through.

It meant showing up, no matter how tired you felt—finishing the task even if your body begged for rest, ignoring distractions, and outworking everyone, being the kind of person who never lets up.

This is the image we carry: discipline as internal pressure, applied over time.

But in a world where our attention is constantly pulled from the outside, where distraction is not a personal failing, but a design feature of the systems we live in, discipline begins to look different. It's no longer about how hard you can push yourself. It's about how you can *protect yourself.*

Which means the real discipline now? Boundaries.

Not the kind of boundary that's about being rigid or unkind. Not an excuse to isolate or avoid responsibility. But the kind that quietly, steadily says: I know what matters. And I'm not available for everything else.

Boundaries are how you build focus into the structure of your life.

Because if you don't choose where your attention goes, someone else will. If you don't say no to noise, noise will find its way in. If you don't carve out the time and space for deep work, your calendar will fill itself with shallow demands that look important, but leave you empty.

That's what makes boundaries hard; they often require you to disappoint someone in the short term to protect your long-term capacity to contribute something real.

And in many places, especially in workplace culture, that's misunderstood.

Saying no can look like resistance. Like you're not a team player. Like you're difficult, or unavailable, or too slow. We've been conditioned to equate availability with value. To be open, reachable, flexible, and responsive. We apologize for taking time to think. We feel guilty for protecting our energy.

But here's the truth: without boundaries, there is no depth.

If your day is dictated entirely by incoming requests, you are not working; you are reacting. You are a relay switch, a messenger, a human notification center. Even if you're checking things off a list, the real work, the kind that requires sustained thought, doesn't stand a chance.

To do deep work consistently, you must become someone who knows when and how to say no.

That might mean saying no to a last-minute meeting request. No to checking email during your peak focus hours. No to keeping Slack open while you write. No to context-switching every time someone wants a quick favour. Not because you're selfish, but because the only way to offer something valuable is to protect the state in which you create it.

Boundaries aren't walls. They are architecture.

They shape the space inside your mind. They give your best work a place to unfold, instead of being trampled by the endless shuffle of tiny demands. And they remind everyone around you, including your team, family, and clients, that your time and attention are not infinite resources.

Of course, boundaries don't always land smoothly.

You might get pushback. Raised eyebrows. Subtle judgments. But the more you practice them, the more people begin to adapt. You teach them how to engage with you. You show, through quiet consistency, that your no isn't rejection, it's respect. It's you choosing to give your *best*, not just your fastest.

And eventually, that becomes trusted.

There's something powerful about someone who doesn't scramble. Someone who doesn't reply out of panic. Someone who creates their days with intention, rather than chaos. Not someone unreachable, but someone who *knows what they're reaching for*.

That is what a boundary protects.

It's not a sign of weakness. It's a sign that you're working on something too important to interrupt.

That you value your thinking enough to defend it.

That your presence, when offered, is whole, and not a scattered fragment given out of obligation.

In this way, boundaries become the new discipline. Not because they're easy, but because they're necessary. They require clarity. They require courage. They require that you decide, again and again, what matters most, and then act accordingly.

This is not about perfection. There will be days when you have to flex, when life is loud, when boundaries bend. That's okay. What matters is that you keep returning. That you treat focus not as something to squeeze in, but something to *build for*.

That you stop waiting for permission and instead begin protecting your mind as if it mattered, because it does.

And not just for productivity.

But for peace.

For presence.

For the quiet, steady dignity of choosing how you spend your time, rather than being paid by everyone else's plans.

# Chapter 35: Resisting Digital Conformity

You don't remember exactly when it started.

You installed one tool because your team used it. Another reason is that your friend swore by it. You joined the chat, created the profile, and opened the account. You didn't think much of it. Everyone else was doing the same. It felt efficient, normal, modern. Over time, your phone has become cluttered with apps. Your desktop bloomed with shortcuts. Notifications multiplied.

Now, you can't seem to get through a single hour without something blinking, buzzing, or asking for a response.

This is the quiet pressure of digital conformity, the subtle but powerful expectation that you will use the same tools, respond the same way, live at the same pace as everyone else. To be professional, informed, or productive, you must also be *available*. Not just reachable, but constantly receptive. To emails. To messages. To updates. To every alert the world throws your way.

But the truth is, most of these tools weren't designed with your mind in mind. They weren't built to help you think clearly or work deeply. They were built for collaboration at scale, which often means compromise. Which often means interruption.

The problem isn't that tools exist. The problem is that we've stopped questioning which ones *belong*.

Digital conformity tells you that if everyone else is in the group chat, you should be too. If your colleagues check their email constantly, you should do the same. If a new app becomes popular, you're behind if you don't download it. And so your digital environment grows, not out of intention, but out of momentum.

But momentum is not wisdom.

Just because a tool is widely adopted doesn't mean it deserves space in your life. Just because everyone's using it doesn't mean it serves your attention. Just because it helps someone else doesn't mean it helps *you*.

And this is where resistance begins.

Not as defiance. Not as detachment. But as discernment.

It's the quiet, difficult choice to live differently from the digital norm. To not respond immediately. Do not join every channel. Do not treat your brain like a shared workspace. It's the decision to use tools with intention instead of letting tools shape your intention.

This requires an uncomfortable kind of honesty. You have to ask what each app *does* to your mind. Not just what it claims to do, but what it creates, what it interrupts, what it pulls you away from. Does it support the thinking you want to do? Does it respect your boundaries? Does it add clarity, or just more noise to manage?

If not, then you have a choice.

You can opt out. You can choose fewer platforms. You can communicate on your terms. You can delay your replies. You can remove the apps that fragment your attention, regardless of their popularity. You can work offline, even if everyone else is online.

You can be unreachable for an hour, or three, or an entire morning, without guilt.

That is how digital resistance begins, not by going off-grid, but by *thinking for yourself.*

And yes, people may notice. You might be slower to respond. You might miss a trend, a ping, or an internal meme. But what you'll gain is something rarer: continuity. The ability to follow a single thread of thought from beginning to end. The ability to stay with a problem long enough to find an elegant solution. The ability to finish something that matters.

That doesn't mean you isolate. It means you stop sacrificing your brain to a culture of constant communication.

It means you stop proving your worth through digital presence.

You don't need to comment on everything. You don't need to "stay in the loop" if the loop is a whirlpool. You don't need to adopt every tool to do meaningful work. The opposite is usually true. The less time you spend *managing* tools, the more time you have to *use* them well, or to avoid them entirely, and think.

Because thinking, not checking, is what creates value.

But thinking is invisible. And digital conformity rewards what's visible. Who's typing? Who's active? Who's posting? Who's pinging? It punishes stillness. It makes presence a metric.

So, if you want to work differently, your job is to stop chasing the optics of productivity and reclaim the *conditions* of real contribution.

That begins by redesigning your digital life with a focus in mind.

Audit your tools, not by how powerful they are, but by how much attention they demand. Turn off the features you don't need. Remove the ones that hijack your time. Use do-not-disturb like your work depends on it, because it does.

Treat your apps like coworkers: if one interrupts you every five minutes, that's a bad fit.

It's not radical to resist digital conformity. It's responsible.

Because your attention is not on a group project, your focus is not on public property. Your value doesn't depend on being constantly connected.

It depends on what you create when you're finally left alone long enough to go deep.

And that solitude, rare, unfashionable, essential, is where real work begins.

# Chapter 36: The 90-Minute Focus Window

You don't need eight hours of deep focus a day.

Your brain can't give you that. Not because you're weak or lazy or undisciplined, but because that's not how your body was designed. Human attention isn't a faucet that flows evenly from sunrise to sunset. It's more like a tide: it rises and falls. It surges, then recedes. And if you learn to work with those rhythms instead of against them, you don't need more time; you need the *right* time.

That's the insight behind the 90-minute focus window.

Your brain operates in cycles, biological patterns known as ultradian rhythms. These cycles, typically lasting about 90 to 120 minutes, govern your ability to concentrate, solve problems, and create. During the first phase of the cycle, your energy rises, your focus sharpens, and your thinking becomes more fluid. Then, like clockwork, it dips. You feel restless, distracted, and sluggish. That's not failure. That's biology.

The mistake most people make is trying to power through the dip. They push, hustle, and re-caffeinate. They switch tasks, check messages, and open new tabs. But in doing so, they flatten their productivity. They dilute the peak moments. They end up working longer but producing less.

The more innovative approach is to *build around the rise*.

To identify your brain's peak window and protect it like gold.

That window is usually ninety minutes. Not too short, not too long. Just enough time to go deep, but not so long that fatigue turns focus into fog. If you use it well, it can change your entire day.

You don't need a perfect schedule to find it. Just pay attention to your energy. When do you feel mentally alive? When do you hit flow without trying? For many people, it's mid-morning, after the day has begun, but before the world has fully claimed you. For others, it's late at night. It doesn't matter when it is. What matters is that you *find it* and then stop giving it away.

That means no meetings. No emails. No shallow work. No multitasking.

It means sitting down with one task, one goal, one tab, and *staying there*.

You won't feel it immediately. Focus doesn't rush in the moment you decide to work. There's a slope to it—a few minutes of resistance. Then something softens. You forgot the clock. The page pulls you in. You stop hearing the background noise. You become, for a brief stretch, completely present.

This is what most people crave, but few people experience. Not because it's rare. But it requires space. You have to stay long enough for the brain to drop in. You have to make it past the first wave of boredom and fidgeting. You have to shut the door, literally or figuratively, and not open it until you're done.

The 90-minute window is your creative container.

And like all containers, its strength is in its shape. It permits you to stop *trying* to focus and *let yourself* concentrate. You don't have to stretch your willpower across an endless day. You have to show up fully for an hour and a half.

Then, just as importantly, you *rest*.

That's the part most people skip. They think the goal is to stack one 90-minute sprint after another. But your brain needs recovery. That dip after the peak? It's not laziness. It's a repair.

It's where integration happens. It's your system saying, "That was good. Now give me space to absorb it."

So you pause. You walk. You breathe. You do something undemanding. You step away from the screen. You let your brain defrag.

Then, if needed, you return. Not to grind, but to go deep again, from a place of clarity.

Two well-protected 90-minute windows a day are enough to do work that moves your life forward. Not just maintenance work. Not just checklists. But original thinking. Complex decision-making. Craft. That's three hours of actual presence, a luxury in the modern world, but entirely possible if you're willing to design for it.

Because that's what this chapter is really about: design.

Focus isn't something you summon in chaos. It's something you *prepare for*. You build the conditions that allow it to arrive. You block the time. You eliminate the noise. You commit to a task that matters. You stop asking your brain to do six things at once and give it the chance to do *one thing well*.

That one thing? It doesn't have to be world-changing. It just has to matter to *you*.

You write the page. You sketch the plan. You solve the problem. You edit the draft. You reflect. You build. You sit with something that needs your full presence, and you *give it*.

That's the win. Not the output. The attention.

Because it's the attention that will shape what you create.

And it's that attention, sustained for ninety minutes a day, that can reshape your entire relationship to work.

# Chapter 37: One Screen at a Time

There's a quiet kind of tension that lives in your body when you're trying to do too many things on too many screens at once.

It starts small. You open your laptop to write a report, but your email is open too. Your phone buzzes beside you. You glance at it, just for a second. A group thread has lit up. You don't respond, but you read it. Then a notification from a calendar app pops up on your desktop. Your mind flickers. You try to refocus, only to remember that one tab is still loading. You open another. By now, the thread of thought you were following is gone.

Nothing exploded. No real crisis happened. But you feel it, the drain. The splintering. A slow unravelling of mental presence.

This is the cost of the modern default: too many screens, layered too closely, all demanding pieces of your mind.

You probably don't think about it much. It's normal. Everyone does it. It feels productive to move quickly between devices, to respond in real time, to scan, switch, reply, and scroll. But that normalcy is precisely the danger. Because what we've normalized is a form of self-fragmentation.

The human brain didn't evolve for this kind of interface stacking.

We evolved to attend deeply to one thing at a time. To walk through a forest, alert to sound and movement. To listen carefully to a voice across a fire. To focus on shaping a tool or weaving a pattern. Our attention was built for immersion, not fragmentation. And yet we now spend most of our cognitive hours flickering across windows, juggling devices, peering at multiple digital surfaces within the exact moment.

You don't even notice it happening until you stop.

Until you turn off the second screen, or move your phone to another room. Or close every tab but one. At first, it feels bare. You might even feel anxious, like something's missing. But after a few minutes, something unexpected happens: your mind begins to settle.

Your thoughts stop bouncing. You hear yourself think again. You remember what you were trying to do in the first place.

That's the power of working with one screen at a time.

It's not a gimmick. It's a neurological alignment. A way of reducing cognitive load, not just by removing distractions, but by simplifying the landscape of your attention. Each open device creates a new potential demand. A new set of possible actions. A new way to be pulled. And your brain, even if you aren't aware of it, is constantly managing that pull.

When you choose one screen, you send a different signal: there is nowhere else to go. Just this. Just here.

You don't need to be extreme about it. You're not becoming a digital monk. You're just reintroducing a sequence where chaos used to live. You're permitting yourself to move slowly and thoroughly, from one thing to the next.

Because here's what no one tells you about multitasking across devices: it doesn't just reduce your performance, it reduces your memory. You retain less of what you read. You solve problems less effectively. You interpret signals less accurately. Not because the tasks are too complex, but because your mental bandwidth is leaking across surfaces.

So, start small.

If you're writing, close your browser.

If you're on a video call, silence your phone and turn it face down.

If you're reading, close your laptop.

If you're thinking, really thinking, make the room reflect that choice. Clean desk. One notebook. One screen. Nothing whispers from the corner.

You don't need more tools to focus. You need fewer open loops.

And yes, it will feel strange at first. There's a kind of withdrawal that happens when you reduce screen hopping. You'll catch yourself reaching for your phone to *do something*, even if there's nothing you need. That reflex isn't about need. It's about momentum. You're breaking a loop your brain has rehearsed thousands of times: boredom → reach → swipe.

Breaking that loop is part of the work. Not because boredom is a problem, but because boredom is where thinking begins. When you remove the second and third screens, you let boredom breathe. You allow space to return. And in that space, your original mind reappears.

Not the mind shaped by algorithmic interruption. The mind that belongs to you. This is not nostalgia. Its design.

It's reclaiming the experience of undivided attention, not to be pure or ascetic or virtuous, but because it works. Because one screen, used deeply, will produce more meaningful output than three screens skimmed in panic. Because presence, once restored, becomes addictive in a good way.

Because the brain, finally, gets to do what it was built for: to attend. Fully. Thoughtfully. Without escape routes, every five seconds.

So, try it. Not forever. Just for one project. One block of time. One morning. One screen.

Watch how your breathing changes. How your posture shifts. How your thinking gets clearer, then deeper, then quieter.

Watch how the anxiety begins to fade, not because your life got easier, but because your mind stopped trying to be everywhere at once.

Watch how, maybe for the first time all day, you feel like yourself again.

# Chapter 38: The Sabbath Principle

There was a time when rest was built into life, not as a luxury, but as a rhythm.

One day out of seven, the world slowed down. Not just spiritually, but physically. Shops closed. Work stopped. Streets emptied. There was space, for once, to be human in a different way. The calendar itself acknowledged that we were more than what we produced. It offered not just a break, but a boundary.

That's what the Sabbath was meant to be. A pause. A deliberate cessation. A time to remember that you are not what you do. That your value isn't tied to output. That the machine of the world can stop, at least briefly, and you'll still be whole.

You don't need to be religious to need that.

You probably need it more than ever.

Because the machine doesn't stop now, the modern world doesn't pause. Notifications don't recognize Sunday. Emails don't sleep. The algorithm doesn't rest. The clock, once something we checked occasionally, now lives in our hands, whispering its demands day and night. We live in a state of low-grade urgency, where stopping feels irresponsible.

But what if stopping was the most responsible thing you could do?

What if rest wasn't escape, but resistance?

The Sabbath Principle is not about dogma. It's not about rules. It's not about worship, unless you want it to be. It's about rhythm. About reclaiming a day, or a portion of one, as something untouched by urgency. A space that doesn't serve the hustle. A space to become whole again.

It doesn't have to be a full day. Even half a day, consistently protected, can begin to shift something in you. The key is not the duration, it's the boundary. This is time that is not optimized, not checked, and not monetized, gamified, or posted. Time that belongs only to itself.

That means: no email. No work tools. No productivity apps. No silent planning under the surface. Just rest. Real rest. Not collapse, not exhaustion, not recovery from burnout, but the kind of rest that reminds you what it feels like to be *alive*, not just useful.

This kind of rest doesn't come naturally anymore. Most people don't know how to do it. When the moment of quiet comes, they reach for their phones. They scroll. They plan. They organize. They look for something to fill the gap. Because the gap feels unfamiliar. The silence feels threatening. Rest, unpracticed, becomes uncomfortable.

That's why it must be practiced.

You start slowly. You don't wait until you're burned out. You don't treat rest as a reward for surviving the week. You treat it as the pattern from which everything else flows. You schedule it *first*, not last.

Because rest isn't the opposite of work, it's what makes work possible.

Your mind is not a battery to be drained and recharged overnight. It's a living system that thrives in cycles. High output requires high recovery. Not just sleep, but spaciousness. Not just vacation, but regular, intentional intervals of no.

The Sabbath Principle serves as a container for that number.

It's what keeps you from slipping into the cult of constant accessibility. It permits you to disconnect without apology. It tells the world: I'm not available right now, because I'm a person, not a platform.

And over time, it begins to heal something.

It restores a kind of trust in yourself, in time, in the possibility that everything necessary doesn't need to happen *right now*. It reminds you what your mind feels like when it isn't bracing against the next demand. It lets you touch something slower, quieter, older than the feed.

That slowness? That quiet?

It's where clarity begins.

Most of the problems people bring to their desks on Monday could be solved more easily if they had truly rested on Sunday. The decision that feels impossible after a week of cognitive load suddenly becomes obvious in stillness. The creative idea that wouldn't come on Friday arrives, unannounced, during a walk. Not because you pushed harder, but because you finally let go.

This is what most productivity advice misses. It treats humans like leaky machines. It talks about optimization, not restoration. But no one ever optimized their way into joy. No one ever hacked their schedule into pieces.

Peace is chosen.

And it's hard to choose when everything around you is still moving.

That's why it matters to stop together.

If you live with others, such as family, roommates, or a partner, make the Sabbath Principle a shared experience. Create a pocket of time where you all agree: no work. No screens. No pressure. Just time together or time alone, but entirely yours. Time that doesn't answer to a clock or a ping.

It doesn't need to be perfect. You'll check your phone sometimes. You'll slip. That's okay. The goal isn't performance, it's rhythm.

And rhythm is built slowly, over time. What matters is the return that you keep coming back to, the pause that you treat as stillness, not as absence, but as something full.

Full of life. Full of self. Full of the kind of presence you didn't realize you were starving for until it returned.

That's the Sabbath. Not a rule. A remembering.

# Chapter 39: Thinking Is Not Wasting Time

You sit at your desk. There's nothing open but a notebook and a pen. No tabs. No messages. No meetings. Just silence, and the slow turning of thought.

You're not typing. You're not moving. You're staring out the window, or at the page. Something stirs, but it hasn't landed yet. A problem floats at the edge of clarity. A decision you haven't made. A sentence that won't quite form. You're thinking.

And almost immediately, a voice in your mind asks, *Shouldn't you be doing something?*

Because that's what we've learned: that if it isn't visible, it isn't valuable. If there's no output, there's no progress. If we're not actively producing, typing, talking, checking, or clicking, we're wasting time.

But thinking is not a pause in productivity.

Thinking *is* productivity.

Not the shallow kind, not the fast-moving kind, not the tidy check-it-off kind, but the kind that creates meaning. That solves problems before they start. That makes better decisions. That prevents rework, panic, and rushed solutions. The type of thinking that makes work *worth* doing in the first place.

And we've almost forgotten how to do it.

Modern work doesn't reward reflection. It rewards motion. The faster you move, the more you appear to be contributing. The more you communicate, the more you seem involved. Meetings multiply. Messages fly. Dashboards update. Everyone looks busy.

But busyness is not clarity.

And the people who appear slow, who take a day to respond, who pause before speaking, who stare at the ceiling before beginning, are often the ones doing the *real work* of thought and not reacting and not scrambling. But processing. Connecting. Distilling.

The irony is that a lack of that kind of thinking has created most of the problems people are racing to fix.

A plan was hastily devised without foresight. A product was shipped before it was ready. A communication was sent before it was understood. A decision made too quickly, without full context. And then hours, sometimes days, are spent cleaning up the consequences.

But what if we normalized the opposite?

What if you didn't have to justify the time you spent staring out the window?

What if thinking were treated like a legitimate task?

Because it is.

Thinking is what happens when you give the mind enough space to catch up to itself, when you resist the urge to fill every gap, when you let ideas simmer instead of yanking them to the surface half-formed. When you listen to the layers of a problem instead of rushing to solve the loudest part.

This kind of mental processing has a rhythm. It can't be rushed. It resists multitasking. It often looks like nothing is happening. But under the surface, synapses are connecting. Ideas are arranging themselves. Conflicting intuitions are being tested. Patterns are emerging.

And then, almost without warning, the insight appears. A phrase you've been missing. A solution that makes the others unnecessary. A question that reframes everything. That's not magic. It's attention, protected long enough to deepen.

The difficulty is that it often feels inefficient.

You can spend forty minutes in thought and come away with a single sentence. You can walk for an hour and realize you've only made one mental step forward. And that feels, at first, like failure.

But that one sentence? That one step?

It might be the thing that saves you six hours of editing, or a dozen rounds of clarification, or a costly mistake down the road. And even if it doesn't, it reminds you of something more profound: that thinking is how we stay connected to our judgment.

In a world full of templates, advice, shortcuts, and prompts, it's easy to outsource your decisions.

It's easy to Google your way through a dilemma, or copy someone else's process, or follow the most upvoted opinion. But nothing is more dangerous than losing the thread of your thought, than forgetting how to trace an idea to its source and test it against your experience.

Deep thinking is how you remember what you believe.

And there is no substitute for that.

So how do you reclaim it?

You begin by making time for it *on purpose*. You schedule thinking time just as you would a meeting. You don't wait until everything else is done. You protect it. You clear space for it, not just in your calendar, but in your environment.

You silence notifications. You close the laptop. You leave your phone in another room. You walk. You write without performing. You sit in silence, not because you're avoiding work, but because *this is the work.*

You endure the discomfort of slowness.

The blank page. The unformed idea. The doubt that creeps in when nothing happens right away. And you stay. Because staying, without rushing, without checking, is what builds the muscle most people lack in a distracted world: the ability to think through complexity.

Don't scan it. Do not outsource it. Think it.

And in that stillness, you start to remember how much intelligence lives inside you, quietly, patiently, waiting for your permission to emerge.

# Chapter 40: Making Focus a Family Value

Focus is not just a personal habit; it's a cultural inheritance.

If you've ever watched a child at play, truly immersed, kneeling in dirt, building something with utter seriousness, you've seen what undivided attention looks like before the world interrupts it. There's no hurry. No audience. No attempt to multitask. Just the simple joy of presence. Of doing one thing, for no other reason than it matters to them.

But somewhere along the way, that purity begins to fray.

Devices are introduced. Routines accelerate. Notifications arrive. Conversations shorten. The grown-up world comes rushing in with its alerts, deadlines, and constant connectivity. And without meaning to, we teach them what we absorbed: that to be successful is to be reachable. To be relevant is to be reactive. To be grown-up is to be busy.

If we're not careful, the culture of distraction becomes a legacy we pass on without thinking.

But it doesn't have to be that way.

Focus, like kindness, like gratitude, is a value we can teach. Not by lectures. Not by rules. But by how we live. By what we protect. By what we model. And it begins with the most brutal truth of all: you cannot teach your children to value attention if you've already given yours away.

That doesn't mean becoming a perfect parent, partner, or sibling. It means being *present*. It means showing them, again and again, that undivided time is possible and precious. That they are worth your full gaze. Those conversations deserve pauses. That presence can exist without a second screen.

Start.

Pick one meal a day where phones aren't allowed at the table, not as punishment, but as an invitation. To listen. To notice things you might otherwise miss. To remember that the people in front of you are real, and breathing, and layered in ways no scroll will ever reveal.

Create rituals of quiet, especially for younger kids. Time to read, or draw, or stare out the window. Time that isn't scheduled or optimized. A time when it's okay to be bored, because boredom is how imagination returns.

And perhaps most importantly, narrate your focus.

Say it aloud: "I'm going to close the laptop now so I can finish this." Or, "I need twenty minutes with no interruptions, and then I'm all yours." Children, even teenagers, learn more from tone and consistency than from any advice you could give. If you protect your attention with care, they'll notice. And they'll begin to wonder if maybe that's something they can do too.

Of course, they live in a different world.

Their digital reality is not going away. Your job isn't to shield them from it entirely; it's to give them tools to survive it with their minds intact. That means letting them struggle sometimes. Let them experience what it feels like to be overstimulated, then gently offer alternatives, not as judgment, but as an experiment.

Teach them that turning off the device isn't punishment, it's a way of getting themselves back.

Model boundaries, not as walls, but as acts of care. Let them see you take a walk without your phone. Let them see you close the computer at a reasonable hour. Let them see you rest on purpose. Let them hear you say no to something good so that you can protect something better.

And when you fail, which you will, admit it. Tell them when you got pulled into the scroll. Tell them how it made you feel. Laugh at yourself. Be honest. Not perfect, just honest.

Because focus isn't a badge, it's a relationship.

And like any relationship, it's built on trust, not fear.

In a family, that trust is built through rhythm. Through consistency. Through moments that say, without needing to be explained: we pay attention here. We care about each other enough to pause. We believe that depth matters more than speed.

Even if your family is just you and your partner, even if you live alone but influence a web of people through work, friendship, or community, this still applies.

Because presence is contagious.

When one person slows down, others start to breathe differently. When one person listens without multitasking, conversations stretch. When one person refuses to let the frantic pace of the world dictate the tone at home, a new tempo emerges. Slower. Quieter. Deeper.

That's not just good for focus.

That's good for love.

Because love, at its root, is undivided attention.

And in a distracted world, there is no greater gift you can give your family than your full presence, again and again, in small and steady ways. The kind of presence that says: I'm here. I see you. Nothing else is more important right now.

Because in that moment, nothing else is.

# Part V: A Life That Can Hold Attention

## Chapter 41: Attention as Identity

You are what you pay attention to.

That idea might sound poetic at first, maybe philosophical. But it's not a metaphor. It's a neurological, emotional, and personal truth. The patterns of your attention shape the structure of your brain. They deepen some neural pathways and let others fade. They determine what you notice, what you value, and what you react to. Over time, what you habitually attend to becomes your filter for reality.

And your filter becomes you.

Not overnight. Not in one scroll or decision. But across thousands of micro-moments, unnoticed but accumulating. You focus on outrage, you become tense. By focusing on beauty, you become more observant. When you focus on scarcity, you feel more fear. You concentrate on depth; you start to crave stillness.

Every glance, every mental tab, every tiny choice about what to read or ignore or re-read is part of the architecture of identity. Your mind builds around what you feed it.

And in the digital age, this becomes more than personal.

Because the inputs are relentless.

Every app wants a piece of you. Every platform tailors itself to hold your gaze. And the algorithms don't care about truth or nuance or quality; they care about engagement. They show you what keeps you clicking, whether or not it's what you'd choose in a moment of stillness. Over time, this shapes not just your preferences but your personality. Without realizing it, you become someone who reacts faster, scrolls longer, and checks compulsively. Not because you're weak, but because attention is being pulled instead of placed.

But that's not the end of the story.

Because attention, though fragile, is also resilient.

You can reclaim it. Slowly. Consciously. You can begin to ask the most straightforward, most challenging question: *What am I giving my mind to?*

Not just in theory, but in practice. When you open your phone. When you walk into a room. When you read. When you listen. When you choose what kind of noise fills your home. What kind of words fill your conversations? What type of content echoes in your head when the screen goes dark?

Because this is the quiet truth no one sells: your attention is your most powerful creative act.

It's the thing you use to shape your day, your relationships, your inner world. It's what makes something matter. It's what turns the vague into the real. And it's the foundation of who you become over time.

You can't outsource that. You can't automate it. You can't let someone else direct it for too long without consequence. Because if you give it away enough times, you wake up one day and realize you've become someone you didn't choose.

That's the risk of attention drift.

And that's why this final part of the journey matters.

This isn't just about productivity anymore. It's not even about focus in the traditional sense. It's about *living a life that can hold attention*. A life not constantly pulled by noise. A life that makes room for presence. For wonder. For ideas that unfold slowly. For conversations that go deeper than schedules allow. For moments that don't need to be captured to be real.

A life that's not always asking, *What's next?*, but one that can pause and say, *This.*

This moment.

This task.

This person.

This breath.

Because that is where identity begins, not in the grand declarations, but in the sustained choice to stay.

So, ask yourself, gently: What's been shaping me?

Where has my attention been leaking?

What would change if I treated focus not just as a skill, but as a form of self-respect?

Because that's what it is.

When you choose what to attend to, you're choosing what to become.

And there's something sacred about that.

# Chapter 42: Presence is the Point

We often treat focus like a tool, something helpful in crossing tasks off a list, completing projects, and reaching milestones. The modern world rewards it in precisely those terms. Focus is seen as a means to an end, a resource to be spent in the service of output. When you can concentrate well, you're told you're more efficient, more competitive, more valuable to your employer or to your followers or your goals. It's a commodity, and like any commodity, it's judged by what it can produce.

But something subtle is lost when we reduce focus to function. The part that doesn't serve a metric. The part that doesn't aim for applause. What we forget is that focus, at its most essential, isn't just about doing, it's about *being*. It is the posture of presence, of allowing your whole mind to meet the moment in front of you, not as a problem to be solved, but as an experience to be lived.

Presence is not flashy. It doesn't announce itself. It often happens when no one's watching. The mind is fully tuned to a conversation with someone you love—the quiet absorption in a book that challenges you in all the right ways. The steady attention given to a child asking a question they've asked before, simply because they want to feel heard. These moments rarely make headlines, but they shape who we are and what it feels like to live inside our skin.

When presence disappears, life begins to blur. Days become noise. You reach the end of a week and wonder what you remember about it. Tasks got done, conversations happened, boxes were checked. But very little sank in. And it's not because nothing important occurred, it's because attention was never fully there to receive it.

This isn't about grand gestures or spiritual enlightenment. It's about the small and ordinary texture of daily life, the way you show up, the way you listen, the way you engage with the world in its real-time unfolding. A life of presence doesn't mean a life of stillness or slowness all the time. It means you're not living elsewhere in your mind while pretending to be here. It means that when you're working, you're not preoccupied with checking something else. That's when you're resting, you're not rehearsing your to-do list. That's when you're with someone, you're not silently managing a dozen mental tabs.

The struggle, of course, is that modern life pulls us in every direction. We're encouraged to split our minds, to answer messages while walking, to scroll while talking, to consume and communicate at the same time. There is no built-in boundary. Screens blur every distinction. And so we normalize partial attention. We pretend to be present, while part of us is always hovering somewhere else, waiting to be summoned by a buzz, a ding, or a reflex.

Over time, this kind of fractured presence leaves a mark. Relationships become shallow, not from malice, but from accumulated absence. Creativity suffers, not from lack of talent, but from never lingering long enough to enter flow. Even rest stops renew us, because we never truly turn off. Our minds become preoccupied with trying to manage everything at once, and as a result, we end up absorbing almost nothing.

To reclaim presence, we don't need to escape our lives; we need to re-enter them, not with heroic discipline or digital purism, but with a commitment to attention as a way of relating. This means treating presence not as a luxury or as something you'll do "after things settle down," but as a practice embedded into the way you move through your hours. You don't need to meditate for an hour to be present. You need to look someone in the eye without glancing at your phone. You need to breathe deeply when you're tempted to rush. You need to finish one task before jumping to the next, not just because it's efficient, but because it's respectful to the work and yourself.

Presence is also not about perfection. You will drift. You'll forget. You'll be halfway through a conversation before realizing you haven't been listening. The goal isn't to be fully engaged every second; it's to notice when you've left and return sooner each time. Like any form of returning, presence grows stronger the more you practice the act of coming back.

The more profound truth is that presence is not a thing we do; it's a quality of being that saturates everything else. It's what makes intimacy real. It's what allows work to become meaningful. It's what transforms routine into ritual. Without it, even the most impressive achievement can feel hollow. With it, even the most mundane moment can become luminous.

This is what's so often missed in our conversations about attention: that focus is not only about finishing things. It's about *feeling* them. Let them unfold with your whole awareness intact. When we treat presence as the point, not just as a tool for getting somewhere else, we allow life itself to regain its shape. We stop treating attention as fuel for achievement and begin to see it as the connective tissue of everything that matters.

What you pay attention to, day by day, is how your life gets built. But the *quality* of your attention, that warm, steady awareness of being here, determines how that life feels from the inside. You can achieve without presence, but it will not satisfy you. You can perform, but you won't remember who you were while doing it. Presence is what turns action into experience. It's what lets you be there for your own life.

# Chapter 43: Slow Is Smooth, Smooth Is Fast

It's a saying borrowed from the world of tactical training, but its truth applies far beyond the field: slow is smooth, smooth is fast. In practice, it means that careful, deliberate movement builds confidence and control, while haste creates more mistakes that must be cleaned up later. When speed becomes the goal, precision suffers. And when precision suffers, speed dissolves into chaos.

In a world obsessed with efficiency, this principle feels almost subversive. Most of us are taught that faster is always better. To win, you need to be ahead. To stay ahead, you need to move constantly, answer quickly, and deliver faster than the next person. So we rush. We reply before we've thoroughly read the message. We act before we've listened. We skim instructions and start building, assuming we'll figure it out along the way. But in our push to be quick, we end up doubling back. Fixing things we botched. Clarifying things we misread. Untangling consequences we didn't think through.

Slowness doesn't mean laziness or lack of ambition. It means moving with enough awareness that your actions land where you intend them to. It means you're not just reacting to what's loudest, you're responding to what's true. And response, in any meaningful work or relationship, takes time. Not endless delay, but enough space to see clearly. Enough pause to gather context, to weigh what matters, to notice what your rushing mind would otherwise miss.

Speed has a cost when it becomes the default. It creates a life of micro-errors, those tiny, unforced mistakes that ripple into miscommunications, misunderstandings, and repeated effort. At work, this might look like sending a deliverable without proofreading, launching a plan without testing it, or trying to juggle five tasks and ending up completing none of them well. In life, it might look like saying something you didn't mean, forgetting a critical moment, or living whole days in a blur of autopilot, too fast to notice the details that would've made it meaningful.

The promise of multitasking, of always hurrying, is that you'll fit more in. And sometimes, superficially, you do. More tasks are touched, more messages are responded to, and more boxes are checked. But when you zoom out, the value is diluted. You touched more things, but how deeply did you feel them? You moved quickly, but where did you go?

Slowness, when chosen, doesn't mean stagnation. It means accuracy. It means you invest your attention with care. It means starting one thing, sticking with it through the middle, and finishing without losing your focus. That's where the smoothness comes in, not just in task execution, but in state of mind. A smooth day, mentally, is one where you're not lurching between windows, jumping between priorities, or apologizing to yourself for not doing anything all the way through.

The irony is that once you start moving smoothly, speed often follows. Not because you're rushing, but because you're not wasting time on recoveries. There are fewer resets, fewer distractions, and fewer minor errors to revisit. And the more often you work that way, the more natural it becomes. The mental habit of staying with something deepens. Your reflexes sharpen, not from urgency, but from familiarity. You know how to get into flow because you've practiced staying there.

To get there, though, you have to resist the momentum of everything around you. The push to hurry doesn't always come from inside. It comes from watching others hurry. From seeing everyone else answer quickly, or speak without pausing, or finish their tasks while you're still on your second paragraph. It's hard not to internalize that pace as the standard. But the pace of the crowd is not a measure of wisdom.

There are places in life where slowness is survival. Emergency medicine. Air traffic control. Negotiations in high-stakes diplomacy. In each situation, the person who remains calm, even under pressure, is the one who saves the most. The lesson is there for the rest of us, even if our jobs aren't dramatic. In daily life, slowness is how you protect clarity, and clarity is how you move with confidence.

This doesn't require a lifestyle overhaul. It doesn't mean doing everything at half-speed. It means noticing your tempo. Catching the moment, you're speeding up reflexively and asking, *Why?* Not all urgency is real. Not all deadlines are sacred. And not every notification deserves your immediate attention.

Sometimes, the most productive thing you can do is to slow down for five minutes before you start a task. To reread the email. To rephrase the question. To sit in silence before you reply. That slowness pays dividends in what follows, because what follows is smoother. And what's smooth becomes sustainable.

That's the quiet secret: sustainable pace outperforms heroic bursts. Not because it wins the race faster, but because it doesn't burn out before the finish line. You're not trying to be fast just today. You're trying to build a way of working and living that you can return to tomorrow, and the next day, and the next, without breaking.

So when the world tells you to go faster, pause. Not to rebel, but to choose. Choose the rhythm that lets you think. Choose the rhythm that allows you to care. Choose the rhythm that leaves room for presence, even in motion.

Because slow, when it's smooth, becomes fast enough. And more than that, it becomes real.

# Chapter 44: Depth Over Noise

There's a kind of silence that settles in your mind when you finally turn off the stream.

Not just the literal noise, the pinging and blinking and background chatter, but the noise behind it. The pressure to know everything. The urge to respond to everyone. The endless pull of content, updates, debates, highlights, warnings, trends. It doesn't shout, but it hums beneath your thoughts, a low-frequency static that keeps you from ever fully landing in the present.

Most people live with that hum so long they stop hearing it. They forget what uninterrupted mental space feels like. Instead of clarity, there's saturation. Instead of connection, there's consumption. The more noise they take in, the less depth they experience.

It happens gradually. You start your day with good intentions. Maybe even with focus. But you check one thing, just quickly, and then something else pulls you: a video, an article, a reaction. Before you know it, your mental state has shifted. You're no longer anchored in your priorities. You've entered the atmosphere of other people's urgency, their opinions, their framing of what matters. You didn't mean to surrender your focus, but it's gone now, scattered across other people's timelines.

And what's worse, you feel behind. Because in a world ruled by volume, there's always something you missed. Some new input. Some update. The noise convinces you that if you check one more time, you'll feel caught up. But you never do.

You don't remember most of what you saw. It didn't nourish you. It just filled the space.

Depth, on the other hand, does something different. It's not as stimulating. It doesn't offer constant novelty. But it gives back more than it takes. Depth builds something in you. It strengthens your thinking. It stretches your understanding. It teaches you to stay, even when the answer isn't immediate, even when the dopamine doesn't hit in the first five seconds.

And depth is not just about ideas. It's about experience. Being fully inside a task, a conversation, a moment. Letting yourself feel the texture of it, not rushing to summarize or share. Choosing the thing that doesn't broadcast as loudly but leaves a lasting imprint. A book that changes the way you see. A walk where your mind finally calms. A project you return to day after day, not for applause but for the quiet satisfaction of watching it take shape.

Choosing depth over noise is hard, not because it's hidden, but because it's quiet. Noise is always louder. Always available. Always updating. It flatters your anxiety and rewards your impatience. But depth requires patience. And patience involves trust. Trust that something valuable is growing beneath the surface, even if no one else sees it yet.

This is the challenge of living in a world designed for distraction. Noise is not an accident. It's the product. Your attention, chopped into pieces, is what drives the economy of the internet. And so the design of almost everything around you is tilted toward fragmentation. Depth must be chosen, not once, but repeatedly, not with guilt or purity, but with conviction.

That might mean closing the app before you finish scrolling. It might mean unsubscribing from things that seem essential but only drain your energy. It might mean reading slower, listening longer, and letting a thought take days to unfold instead of trying to compress it into a tweet.

None of this makes you fall behind. It's how you stay sane. Because noise doesn't make you informed, it makes you reactive. And a reactive mind is not a free mind.

When you build a life around depth, something begins to shift. You feel less hurried. Not because you have less to do, but because your mind isn't constantly being yanked elsewhere. You stop measuring your day by how many things you touched and start asking: *Did I feel anything deeply?*

You also become harder to manipulate. It's much more difficult to sell something to someone who takes time to think. Someone who can pause long enough to ask, *Is this true? Is this useful? Is this mine?* The more depth you cultivate, the less you chase urgency manufactured by others.

Depth is protective.

It grounds you in your own pace, your questions, your way of seeing. It doesn't make you smarter in the IQ sense; instead, it makes you wiser in the *time spent paying attention*. You begin to feel the difference between novelty and meaning. Between stimulation and resonance. Between what's loud and what lasts.

And what lasts is never noise.

What lasts is built through slowness, through presence, through returning to something over and over until it yields something you couldn't see the first time. That might be a piece of writing, a relationship, a spiritual practice, or a long-term goal.

Whatever it is, it will ask something of you that noise never does: your sustained attention.

That is the price of depth, and also its gift.

Because once you've experienced it, even briefly, noise begins to lose its grip. You recognize its emptiness. You feel the drain. And you start to crave something quieter, but infinitely richer—something you can build a life around.

# Chapter 45: The Gentle Mind

It's strange how often we approach our minds as adversaries.

We set alarms, build systems, craft routines, not always to support ourselves, but to contain what we think is flawed or lazy or insufficient within us. We tell ourselves that without constant pressure, we'd fall apart. That we need discipline to conquer distraction, that willpower must override every moment of fatigue, and that the only thing standing between us and focus is our failure to be harder on ourselves.

But pressure doesn't create clarity. And harshness doesn't build focus. What they make is tension. A mind that's always braced, constantly policing itself, always one small slip away from shame.

We call it productivity. But often, it's just stress in disguise.

If you listen closely to the way most people talk about focus, it sounds like war. They fight procrastination. They battle their inbox. They push through burnout. Their mind becomes a battleground, and their body carries the weight of that fight, shoulders tight, sleep interrupted, a nervous system stuck in a permanent state of alert.

This isn't what attention needs.

The mind doesn't focus well under threat. It narrows. It flinches. It protects itself. You might get short bursts of output that way, fueled by adrenaline or fear, but you won't get your best ideas. You won't go deep. You won't linger long enough in silence to hear what you think.

Absolute focus, the kind that sustains and creates and heals, grows in gentleness.

A gentle mind is not a passive one. It's not vague or unfocused or soft in the lazy sense. It is spacious. It is receptive. It knows how to slow down without collapsing. It knows how to rest without guilt. It knows how to begin again, not with punishment, but with patience.

This kind of mind doesn't come naturally to most of us. We were raised in a culture that equates being hard on yourself with being responsible. That tells us the voice of the inner critic is the voice of maturity. That if you're not suffering a little, you must not be trying hard enough.

But if you look at the people who do sustained, meaningful, thoughtful work over time, what you find is not people at war with themselves. You see people who know how to care for their attention. People who step away when they're tired and trust that rest is part of the process. People who forgive distraction, not to excuse it, but to learn from it. People who return, again and again, to the task not with force, but with curiosity.

That return, calm, open, steady, is the mark of a gentle mind.

Gentleness doesn't mean you never struggle. It means you don't turn the struggle into self-hatred. It means you treat your attention like something to be nourished, not bullied. Like something worth protecting, not because it's perfect, but because it's alive.

A gentle mind pays attention to its signals. It knows the difference between effort and strain. It can work hard, sometimes very hard, but it doesn't confuse fatigue with failure. It doesn't make a shame the price of losing focus. And when it inevitably drifts, it simply comes back.

That's what gentleness makes possible: return without drama.

And the more you practice returning in that way, the less energy you waste fighting yourself. You begin to trust that you don't need to white-knuckle your way through every moment. You don't need to be rigid to be committed. You can care deeply without needing to crack the whip.

The voice inside you changes.

Instead of constant critique, you hear questions. What helps me focus? What pulls me away? What rhythm feels natural today? What needs space? What needs structure? These are not the questions of weakness. They are the questions of wisdom.

Because your attention is not a machine, it's not a switch to flip on and off. It's a relationship, and like any relationship, it deepens with kindness. The more gently you treat it, the more it opens up to you. The more it trusts you to come back, again and again, not out of fear, but from devotion.

Gentleness doesn't remove effort. But it changes the tone of effort.

Instead of bracing, you begin to lean. Instead of forcing, you start to listen. Instead of performing for some imagined scoreboard, you begin to inhabit your mind more fully. And in that inhabiting, something rare happens: peace.

Not the absence of noise, but the presence of stability.

And in that stability, focus finds its home.

# Chapter 46: Freedom from Notifications

At first, it feels like silence—a kind of emptiness you're not used to. You reach for your phone, and it doesn't vibrate. You glance at the screen and nothing new appears. You open your laptop and realize no red badges are calling your name. The world, so accustomed to whispering in your pocket every few minutes, has gone quiet.

That quite unnerves you.

Because for so long, notifications have been your heartbeat. Little flashes of validation, urgency, reminders of activity. Even the meaningless ones, like an update from an app you forgot you installed or a promotional ping, brought a kind of comfort. They meant you were in the loop, reachable, relevant. To turn them off is to confront something more disorienting than boredom: the feeling of being alone with your attention.

This chapter isn't about digital detox or abandoning technology. It's about what happens when you reclaim your right not to be interrupted, when you decide, consciously, that your mind belongs to you again.

It started as an experiment. Thirty days without notifications. Not just muting sounds, but removing banners, badges, alerts, vibrations, everything. No visual cues pulling focus. No little red dots reminding you of something you'd supposedly forgotten. The phone still worked. Email and texts still existed. But they were only there when you chose to look. Not the other way around.

The first few days felt like withdrawal. There were moments of phantom buzzing, the muscle memory of checking without thinking. A strange guilt settled in when messages sat unanswered for more than a few minutes. But under the discomfort, something else began to emerge, space.

With no interruptions, time stretched. Tasks that usually felt fragmented began to settle into rhythm. Conversations became more present. Work deepened. Even walking down the street became less frantic. The mind stopped scanning for the following beep, the next tap on the shoulder.

What became clear, almost painfully clear, was how deeply conditioned the body had become to expect interruption. It wasn't just a habit. It was anticipation wired into the nervous system. Even without sound, even without light, the mind kept looking for the next demand.

But as the days went on, that grip loosened.

The phone began to feel less like an appendage and more like a tool. It no longer dictated the cadence of the day. There was no longer a script running in the background telling you to check, check, check. The craving faded. What replaced it was not asceticism, but clarity—a chance to ask, without distraction, what matters.

What emerged, more than anything, was a deep sense of sovereignty. Not just control, but ownership. Your time was your own. Your thoughts could unfold without being hijacked. You could linger in a task, an idea, or a mood without something barging in uninvited. And slowly, you remembered what it felt like to follow a whole thread of thought all the way through.

Of course, the world didn't stop because you stopped checking. Important messages still came. People still found ways to reach you. But very little was truly urgent. Most of what used to feel immediate revealed itself as noise in hindsight: quick reactions, vague nudges, automated reminders. None of them improved your focus. They just interrupted it.

The strange part is that we built this system. Every buzz, every ping, every badge was something we once agreed to, if not consciously, then passively. We said yes to all of it, a little at a time. And slowly, without realizing it, we gave away our right to uninterrupted thought.

Turning it off isn't about disconnecting from the world. It's about reconnecting to your mind. It's about remembering that responsiveness is not the same as responsibility. That you can still care deeply about people, about work, about the state of things, without being on call for all of it, all the time.

The cost of constant connectivity is not just time. Its texture. When alerts pierce every moment, the quality of attention frays. Depth becomes harder to access. Thought becomes more scattered. Even joy becomes more fragile, because it can be interrupted mid-breath by someone else's urgency.

Living without notifications teaches you something important: almost nothing falls apart if you wait. The people who genuinely need you will find you. The rest can sit in silence until you're ready. And in that silence, something powerful begins to grow, attention that is entirely yours.

Not because you isolated yourself, but because you remembered how to *choose*.

# Chapter 47: Attention as a Civic Act

There's a narrow way of thinking about focus, as something purely personal—a matter of self-improvement, of getting more done, of organizing your day. But when you widen the lens, attention becomes something larger, more consequential. It becomes not just a mental resource but a moral and civic one.

Because the way we pay attention doesn't just shape our private lives, it shapes our communities, our conversations, our democracy. It determines what stories get told, what ideas spread, what injustices stay visible, and which quietly disappear. It determines who we listen to and who we ignore.

In that sense, attention is not just a skill. It's a form of participation.

The distracted citizen is easier to influence. Easier to sell to. Easier to divide. When your attention is constantly fragmented, it becomes difficult to engage meaningfully with anything that takes time or context. You skim. You react. You adopt opinions instead of forming them. You become more susceptible to outrage and less equipped for complexity.

It's not because you don't care. It's because caring requires stamina. And stamina involves focus.

There's a quiet but powerful connection between the private discipline of attention and the public good. A society that cannot pay sustained attention cannot think clearly about its future. It can react, mobilize, and shout, but it cannot deliberate. It cannot reflect. And without reflection, there is no real decision-making, only impulse.

We often think of manipulation as something overt, but the most effective manipulation is subtle. It works not by forcing you to believe something, but by shaping what you notice. What appears in front of you. What gets repeated until it becomes familiar. When your attention is guided by algorithms rather than intention, your worldview becomes someone else's design.

Reclaiming your focus, then, is not just about living a better life. It's about becoming harder to deceive. Harder to distract. More capable of asking: who benefits from the way this is being framed? What might be missing? What would I see if I looked more closely, more slowly?

That kind of critical attention is rare in a world built on speed. Most platforms reward speed of reaction, not depth of insight. The faster you respond, the more visible you become. And so we learn, without meaning to, that being informed means being constantly updated. That being engaged means being emotionally activated.

But real engagement is quieter than that. It happens in the moments when you sit with a story long enough to ask what it demands of you, when you hear someone's experience without immediately making it about your own. When you resist the urge to reply and instead choose to understand.

This doesn't mean you have to be a policy expert or a full-time activist. It means understanding that your attention is one of the most powerful tools you have to shape the world around you. What you give time to, what you read, what you share, what you amplify, ripples outward. It teaches others what you think matters.

And it teaches you, too.

Because attention isn't just about seeing the world, it's about forming yourself around it. The people who pay close attention over time develop something deeper than knowledge: they develop discernment. They become better at telling the difference between urgency and manipulation, between popularity and truth, between noise and signal.

In that way, attention becomes a form of resistance. Not loud, not dramatic, but consistent. Every time you choose to pause before reacting, every time you choose to listen all the way through, every time you decide to seek out the full story instead of the headline, you are resisting the forces that want you superficial and distracted.

And you are practicing something essential: the habits of an attentive citizen.

These habits don't show up on productivity dashboards. They don't earn badges. But they matter. They create communities that listen before they judge. They support leaders who think before they speak. They make space for the complicated, the nuanced, the slow-to-understand.

In a time when so much feels chaotic and unstable, it's easy to believe your focus only matters within the walls of your own home or your inbox. But the truth is, every act of attention sends a signal to your children, your colleagues, your neighbours. It says: I choose to stay awake. I prefer to be here. I choose to care, even when it's hard.

And in that caring, something begins to rebuild not just within you, but around you.

# Chapter 48: The World You're Building in Your Mind

Every day, whether we realize it or not, we are shaping an interior landscape.

It happens quietly. The articles we skim, the conversations we replay, the images we absorb, the podcasts we let run in the background, all of it gathers somewhere beneath the surface. Over time, these fragments settle into something more permanent: a set of mental walls and windows, paths and patterns, stories and symbols. The mind becomes not just a container of facts or memories but a *place*, a terrain you return to in stillness, in decisions, in doubt.

And that place, that internal world, becomes the lens through which you experience everything else.

This idea, that you are always building your inner environment, matters now more than ever. Because we are flooded with inputs, the volume of content, opinions, updates, and noise we absorb in a week would have overwhelmed the average person a century ago in an entire lifetime. We take in more than we can process. And yet we rarely pause to ask: *What kind of world am I creating in my mind with all this?*

It's easy to overlook. You might scroll through a news feed and tell yourself nothing stuck. You might binge three episodes of a show and assume you've moved on. But your mind is porous. It doesn't forget as quickly as you do, especially when something is repeated, especially when it carries emotion, especially when you consume it unconsciously.

If you spend your days taking in conflict, outrage, advertising, and comparison, even passively, you start to feel those things even when no screen is in front of you. You begin to interpret silence as a threat—stillness as stagnation. You become more reactive. More restless. Less at home in your thoughts.

But the inverse is also true.

Suppose you begin to choose your inputs, even gently, the mind changes. If you surround yourself with voices that stretch you, ideas that challenge without shaming, stories that nourish instead of inflaming, you begin to feel a different texture inside your thinking. Not immediately. Not all at once. But gradually, you start to recognize what it feels like to be mentally spacious. To feel less hijacked by each new headline. Less tangled in performance. More able to return to stillness without dread.

Because your attention doesn't just shape what you notice, it shapes who you *are* when no one else is around.

That's why this chapter doesn't offer a set of rules for what to read, watch, or follow. It invites you instead to notice the interior space you're living in. To ask: what kind of environment have I built in my mind? Is it crowded? Is it calm? Is it reactive? Is it fertile? Who else lives here with me? What voices echo? Which thoughts feel at home, and which feel foreign?

And then to ask the more complex question: What would I like to grow here instead?

Because the mind is not static, it is not fixed. It is constantly remodelling and always absorbing, discarding, reweaving. You have agency, even if you've forgotten. You can curate what enters. You can prune. You can plant.

This isn't about perfection. It's about becoming a conscious architect. It's about treating your attention like building material.

Every moment of silence you protect, every conversation you choose to deepen instead of deflect, every time you stop scrolling just because you can, those are bricks in the walls of your internal world. Those are the textures of your future thoughts.

And when you do this not as an emergency measure but as a way of life, something remarkable happens. Your inner world begins to support you. Instead of scrambling to create calm from chaos, you find that you've already laid the foundation. Instead of having to claw your way back to focus, you discover that focus is the atmosphere your mind prefers.

Over time, the mental space you've built becomes a kind of refuge. A place where ideas can land. Where clarity can gather. Where not everything has to be solved immediately, and not every open tab needs to stay open forever.

The world outside will always demand your attention. There will always be more to see, more to know, more to be outraged or amazed by. But the world inside, that's yours to shape. That's the space you'll return to every day for the rest of your life.

So build it with care. Fill it with light. Make it quiet enough to hear your thoughts. Make it strong enough to hold your values when the world goes loud again. Not because it's an escape, but because it's home.

# Chapter 49: You're Allowed to Go Quiet

At some point, you begin to wonder whether being reachable all the time is a requirement, or just something you've come to accept without question. You wonder whether the pressure to respond quickly, to be visibly engaged, to maintain a steady stream of output and opinions, is necessary, or whether it's simply a habit dressed up as responsibility.

There's a kind of fatigue that comes not from physical exertion or even mental strain, but from being *perpetually available*. The fatigue of never quite turning off, never quite disappearing, never letting yourself fall off the radar for even a moment. You're online in a hundred small ways, not just digitally but socially and psychologically. You're performing even when you don't mean to. You're reacting even when you're trying to rest.

In this climate, quiet can feel like rebellion.

Not silence as avoidance, but quiet as a conscious shift in posture. As a declaration: I don't need to be visible to be real. I don't need to be loud to be valuable. I don't need to explain every pause, or narrate every thought, or justify every break from the stream.

Going quiet doesn't mean going away. It doesn't mean cutting ties or disappearing from what matters. It means allowing yourself to move without broadcasting. To feel without translating it into something presentable. To learn, to think, to heal, without making that process a performance.

There's power in becoming illegible to the noise around you, in stepping back from the demand to be continually interpreted and understood. Not everyone needs to see you at every stage of your unfolding. Not every insight needs to be packaged. Some things are richer when held privately, allowed to deepen in the dark.

But this isn't easy. The architecture of our lives is increasingly designed around visibility. Metrics, likes, response times, they all point in the same direction: say more, say it faster, keep showing up. There's a low-level panic that creeps in when we step away. Will people forget us? Will we lose momentum? Will our absence be misread?

The more profound fear is often that quiet looks like failure. Like not keeping up. Like letting go of relevance. But what if it's the opposite?

What if quiet is where the real work begins?

There are seasons in life when growth happens underground. When the outward signs of progress disappear, something essential is still taking shape. A shift in how you see. A new kind of clarity, fragile and untested. An idea not yet ready for sharing. A wound not yet healed, but slowly knitting itself together out of sight.

You don't have to explain these seasons. You don't owe the world a constant stream of articulation. Sometimes the most honest thing you can say is nothing at all. Not because you're lost, but because you're listening. Because what's coming next deserves your full attention, and right now, your attention is inward.

Going quiet is not a retreat from life. It's a return to the parts of life that don't thrive under constant exposure. It's how you remember that some of the most sacred things lose their shape when overly explained. Some of the most precious insights only arrive when there's enough space for them to land without competition.

In the quiet, you reencounter your rhythm. You begin to notice when you're tired, not just when it's convenient. You see how your thoughts unfold without commentary. You discover what you miss when the noise subsides, and what you don't.

And when the time comes to re-enter the world of sound, of response, of engagement, you do so with a stronger spine. You're not grasping for attention or signalling relevance. You're grounded. You're speaking from fullness, not from compulsion.

In a world that pressures you to be constantly expressive, going quiet is not failure. It's a craft. Its presence. It's the discipline of listening long enough to know what's truly yours to say.

You're allowed to go quiet.

You always were.

# Chapter 50: A New Myth to Live By

We build our lives around the stories we believe.

Some are spoken out loud. The culture, absorbed through repetition, implies others who lived before we ever chose them. One of the most dominant stories of the modern age has been that of constant productivity: the myth that doing more, faster, with less rest and more access, leads to a life of meaning. That multitasking is a skill to master. That our value lies in our ability to juggle, respond, accumulate, and achieve.

This myth has shaped entire generations. It has filled our calendars and fractured our attention. It has redefined presence as performance. It has taught us to glorify exhaustion, to equate speed with competence, and to wear busyness like a badge of honour. In its shadow, stillness looks lazy. Focus looks inefficient. Depth looks risky.

But myths only endure if we keep living them.

And this one is breaking down.

We feel it in the hollowness that lingers after a day spent racing between tabs. In the frustration of shallow conversations, surface-level work, and evenings filled with screens but absent rest. We feel it in the strange anxiety that something important is slipping past us, even as we stay connected to everything all the time.

We are beginning to understand that doing more isn't the same as living well. That constant input doesn't create clarity. That responsiveness is not the same thing as presence. And that attention is not a resource to be mined; it is the foundation of our capacity to choose, to connect, to create.

What we need now is a new story.

Not a manifesto. Not a productivity method. A myth, not in the sense of something false, but something foundational. A way of imagining the kind of life we want to build. A myth that offers coherence in a time of fragmentation. That dares to center slowness, presence, and care in a world that still worships speed.

Imagine a life where depth is more respected than volume.

Being available isn't proof of importance, but something chosen with intention.

Where conversations unfold without performance, and work is done without distraction.

Where silence is honoured, not as absence, but as the space from which clarity emerges.

Where rest is not a luxury, but a birthright.

Where your value isn't measured by output, but by the integrity of your attention.

This kind of life is not out of reach. But it will not happen by accident. It must be designed, chosen, and protected. It must be practiced again and again, often in quiet defiance of what's expected. It requires not only boundaries and rituals, but a profound reimagining of what success feels like. Not applause, but alignment. Not noise, but resonance. Not presence as a strategy, but as a way of being.

You don't have to abandon ambition to live this way. You don't have to retreat from responsibility or give up on the idea of impact. But you do have to become someone who can focus long enough to ask the better question: *What am I building with my attention?*

Because that is what your life is.

It's not your resume or your follower count or your ability to respond quickly to every demand. It's the sum of what you notice, what you stay with, what you return to, what you let in, and what you let go.

And so, at the end of this book, the invitation is simple but radical: retire the myth of multitasking. Let it go. You don't need it anymore. You never did.

Choose instead a new myth. A life of depth. Of presence. Of attention that reflects not just what the world asks of you, but who you're becoming.

The future belongs to those who can hold their focus long enough to imagine something better.

Now, you can.

# Available Now

Book Two – The Burnout Blueprint: Rewiring Your Life for Energy, Attention, and Meaning

You've learned how to protect your focus. Now it's time to protect your energy.

In a culture that glorifies hustle and rewards exhaustion, burnout isn't a failure; it's a signal. The Burnout Blueprint reveals why your calendar is full, yet your soul feels empty. This isn't about productivity hacks or spa days. It's about understanding the deeper systems —cognitive, cultural, and emotional —that drain you daily.

Using a blend of brain science, ancient wisdom, and modern-day realism, this book will help you redesign your days around rhythms that replenish rather than deplete. You'll learn how to stop running on adrenaline, recognize the early signs of energetic bankruptcy, and create space for work that feels like you.

This is your map out of burnout and toward a life with depth, margin, and meaning.

This book is part of The Deep Work Society trilogy, each of which addresses different dimensions of modern cognitive life: focus, burnout, and tech hygiene.

# About the Author

Written anonymously by a former multitasker who lived the burnout, bought the productivity tools, and still couldn't hear himself think.

The Deep Work Society trilogy was created not to impress, but to invite. Each book is a quiet rebellion against the noise, offered by someone who stepped back, paid attention, and started writing things down.

No name. No brand. Just ideas that might help you remember what it feels like to be present again

# About the Publisher

Welcome to The Book On Publishing

At The Book On Publishing, we believe in rewriting the rules of learning. Whether you're chasing your next big idea, building a better life, or simply curious about what should have been taught in school, you've come to the right place.

We're a platform built for dreamers, doers, and lifelong learners, offering bold, practical books and tools that empower you to take charge of your journey. From real-world skills to mindset mastery, we publish the book on what matters.

No fluff. No lectures. Just what you need to know, delivered with clarity, purpose, and a spark of curiosity.

Start exploring. Start growing. Start writing your story.

Read more at http://thebookon.ca.

# Acknowledgment of AI Assistance

Portions of this book were developed with the support of ChatGPT, an AI language model created by OpenAI. While every word has been carefully reviewed and refined by the author, ChatGPT served as a valuable tool for brainstorming, editing, and structuring ideas. Its assistance helped accelerate the creative process and bring clarity to complex topics.